From Shadows to Serenity

A Soul's Journey

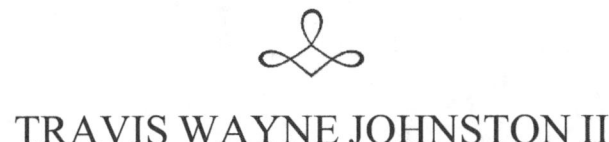

TRAVIS WAYNE JOHNSTON II

Table of Contents

Trepidation Bestowed

The crimson drip that ever flows,

He takes the sip, he who knows,

Eternal life offered from the cursed chalice,

A young hand cut by a knife immersed in malice,

A beast marked with an obsession with the feeble and oppressed,

Never to cease the eternal procession of upheaval and unrest,

The vivacious struggle of a doomed vermin,

Shows the tenacious digestion of the slimy serpent,

He wriggles and writhes, in the muddled water he lies,

Obsessed with his own demise, brought on by ever present pride,

Cursed with a bell that ever scrapes against the ground,

Yet blessed with movement slyly making no sound,

He coils and strikes, he boils the mice,

He sells deceit daily, not once or twice,

A ghost, a specter, a phantom he vanishes,

Power galore yet still he famishes,

No power is enough; he desires far more,

Cower or bluff, your flesh still torn,

Fear him? Certainly, this is smart,

Are you near him? Terror is a start,

You will never see his arrival or even begin to suspect,

Nothing is his rival, he demands complete respect,

Do I describe the devil, the ruler of Hell below?

Do I hide, do I tremble, do I tell you my woe?

Call him the horned master if it relieves, if it gives peace,

But what your scorn is after is what deceives, living in you and me,

This thing I tell you of, this vampire, this affliction,

It'll rip away all you love, drenched in fire, it's your addiction

Haunted by memories of what I've done, what I've had done to me, and what I've seen people do to each other has led me to run blindly down a path without knowing where it would lead. I've been running from myself for years. They say the blind can't lead the blind, otherwise they'll both end up in the ditch. Well, I'll tell you, from my own bitter experience, the Devil isn't blind; he knows exactly where he leads us. Ultimately, I *had* to repeat the same mistakes repeatedly for years, weeping bitterly as years turned into decades. I now solemnly believe that I *had* to. I *had* to so that, with nowhere left to turn, I delved deep within myself. It was in this last analysis that I found the only thing that ever could have relieved me of the bondage of self: my creator. A loving intelligence that created me for a purpose, to do something here on earth, and gave me a reason to live. The world and its people, myself included, with all of our weakness and vices choked out the awareness that I am never alone. I turned to many powers greater than myself to quell my aches and pains, to calm my troubles; they indeed accomplished these lofty goals initially, but in the end, they either delayed my sorrow, prolonged it, or intensified it. I've had many days where I no longer wanted to live. But only one day when I wanted to live desperately but could no longer live with the man I was. That was the day I found God.

Boondock Saint

Navigated a path was taken, but amnesia took hold,
I have coal all around me, but I thought it was gold,
Regardless of what I say, I've lost my way,
How in God's name did I end up in this place?

We suffer oppression through suppression; I digress because I obsess,
I believe you would understand if you could see what I've witnessed,
Ignorance is bliss is an ignorant lie hard to digest,
My refusal to do so creates these words which are blessed,

But they do not emit from my chest, they're divinely inspired,
I pick up my pen and the spirit does the rest, and He doesn't tire,
To become a Boondock Saint, an artist that paints,
The walls with blood of disdain, he is the one who sees it as plain,

No black and white, but paradoxically no color either,
You may think him blind and stupid I can tell you he's neither,
I am thankful of much, that I have been awoken,
So I can share these words which are often unspoken,

I've huffed, I've drank, willing to jam cold metal into my arm,
Anything to protect my fragile ego from truths harm,
So now I hit my knees to show gratitude because I've come so far

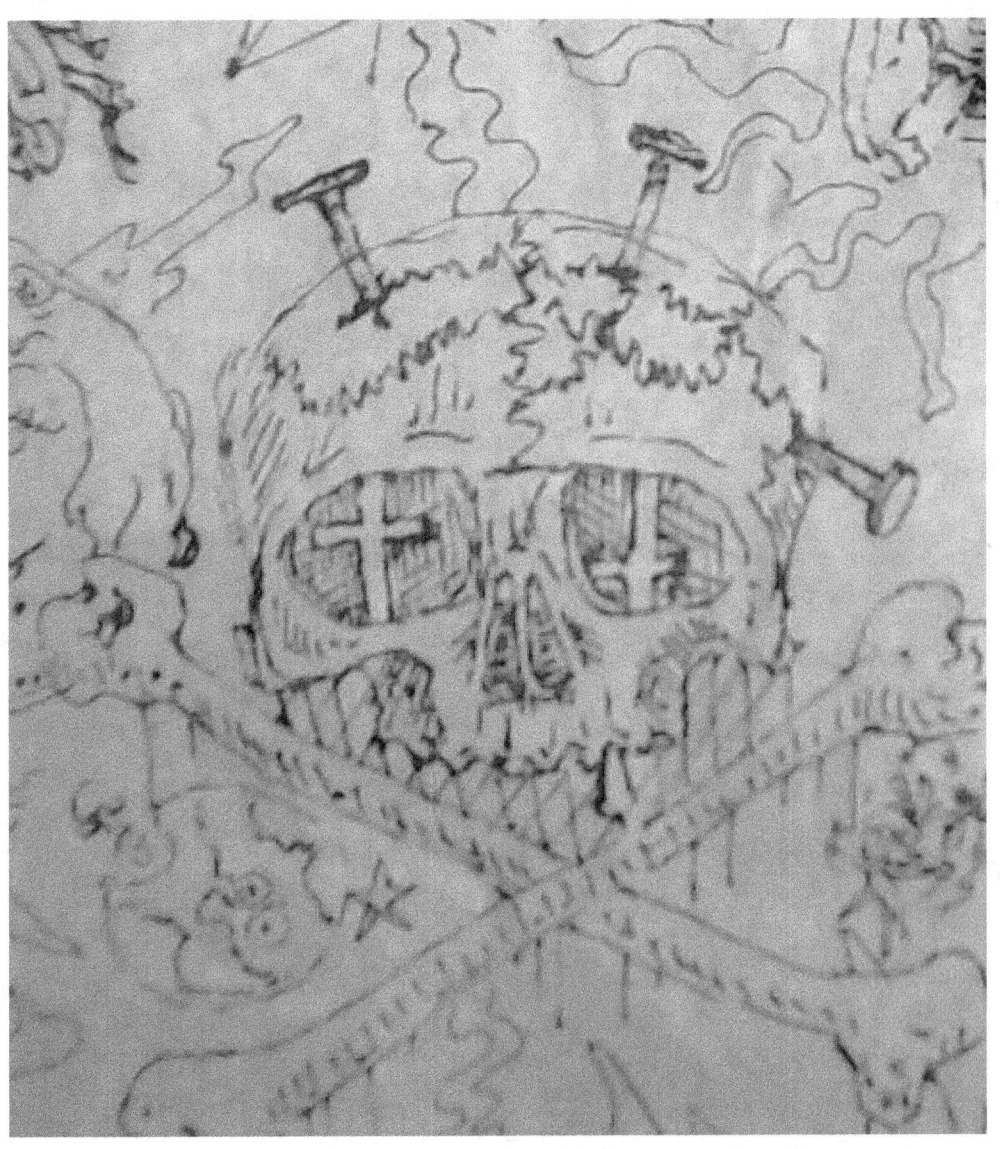

Teeth Seize

Metal rust on the tongue of death,

Settled dust on the plunged blood chest,

Rewind the tape to seek an escape,

Too late, you can't tempt fate,

Once she sees your eyes peering through the haze,

He begins to wheeze as the lie's flames glaze,

Teeth seize as the mother weeps,

Speak!

You fool,

Can't you see?

Silence is cruel,

Clouds pass, sounds last,

Despite the fact they're found in the past,

You want to leave them behind?

It can't happen; they're etched in your mind,

Climb, glare,

A rhymes snare,

Stuck in the bush of a broken soul,

Struck by the rush of a cloaking toll,

Hide in your cloak,

Croak,

Soak in the slime of your crime, they lied,

When they claimed pain lessens in time,

The tome of a lost home is such a heavy load,

Outside of time as if you embody a crow,

Bound by the chains created by a corroding thread,

A crown of pain crowing what she once said,

Love? Does such a thing even exist?

Blood, the same as a shattered kiss,

Reality is something real,

Most of us see it in teal,

Pining for the fantasy in their mind they're designing,

All they end up finding is their own voice is lying,

If I could be close to the end of it all,

Then I would have chosen the fall,

I don't really feel alive unless I'm on the brink,

Unless I feel like I'll die from what I think,

Unless I'm on a leaking ship about to sink,

Unless I need to empty out the sea a bucket at a time,

They say it's a losing battle, that's the point I cry,

Cruelty is a fool's decree,

I reply that it's simply life,

Stop the bleeding while holding the knife

Disgrace

The wasps that talk swarm my head,

The thoughts they brought warm the dead,

Or can be used to warn of impending dread,

Should I have left these words unsaid?

Flies hover over the corpse of my mind,

Perhaps at worse, they seem just fine,

Is their presence indicative of demise?

Or was all this part of the design?

Tell me the truth if you can, or lie to my face,

Hell stitched with glue of sins of the human race,

What else can this be called but a true disgrace?

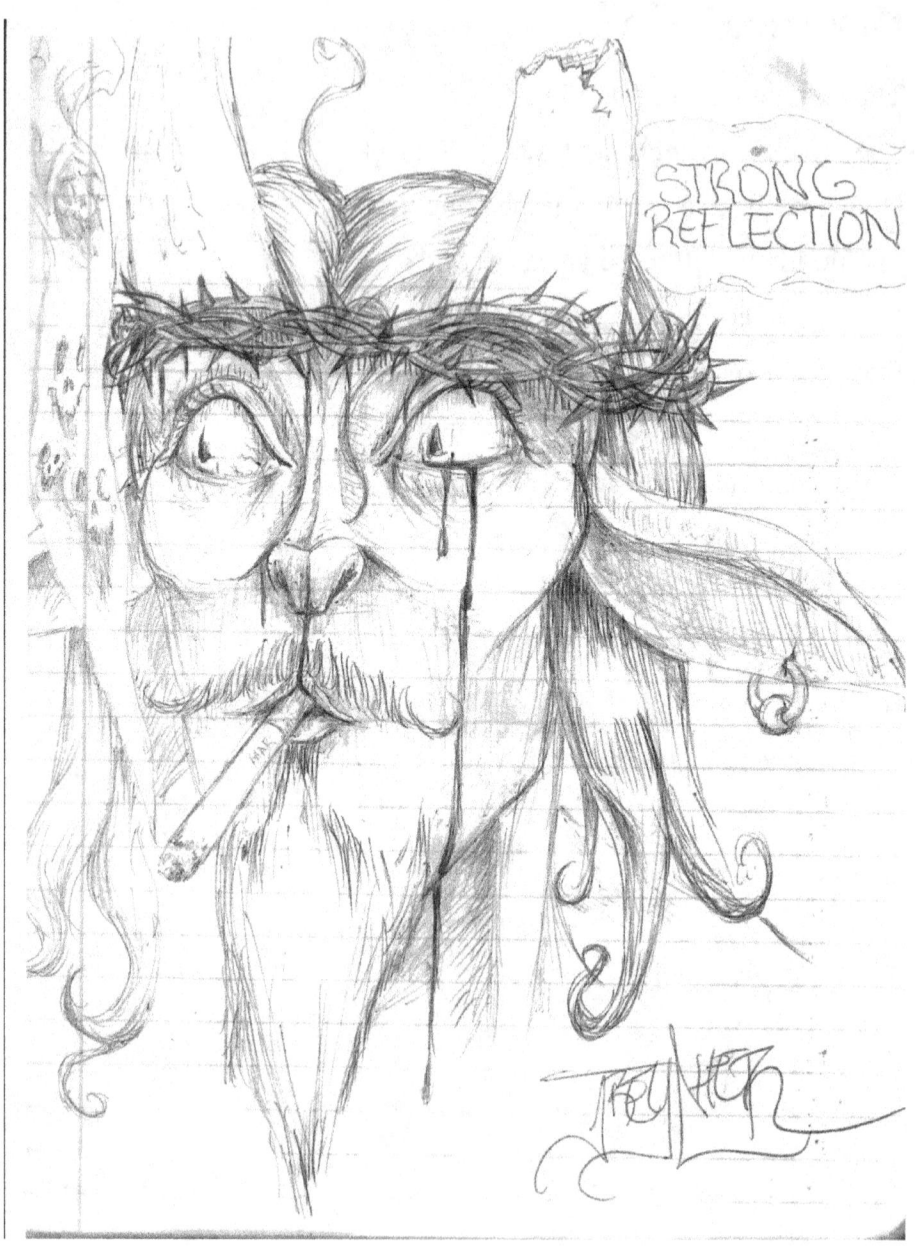

Eternal Slumber

The past brings memories of terror,

The future seems most likely bleak,

Will my last moments be in a snare or,

Will I leave off at the peak?

Each and every decision I make,

Leads to a different set of choices,

Is this a course of collision I undertake?

Will I end up being haunted by voices?

I thought I committed to complete surrender,

So why am I so cautious?

When God's services are always there to render,

My disease likes to shape shift,

How do I remove the inner fool?

Who still thinks he's in control,

I know it's just a sinner's tool,

That takes this eternal heavy toll,

It's in moments like this, so sublime,

With the sun shining on my face,

I know it'll never cease to rise,

Forever set on its own pace,

The basics of all of life,

Are of course far greater than you or I,

The source of all my strife,

Lay in the broken decipher of my eyes,

As I read the words, inspired by God,

I have moments of clarity,

And in the moments angels applaud,

Because I see my own vanity,

My choices are never infinite in number,

It's either in the wrong or in the right,

When I finally reach eternal slumber,

I pray I chose at long last the good fight

On the Cross

Nailed to the cross, he knew the cost,

Yet he remained willing to endure the loss,

They know not what they do, he bellowed aloud,

As they spat and mocked, that vile crowd,

Not all that spectated were vile or mean,

So many wanted his pain to end, this their plea,

Their cries were heard as the Lord shook the earth,

Jesus was our salvation destined from his birth,

When he was removed and his body was taken to be buried,

There were sobs heard from his mother the Virgin Mary,

Although it was simply the start of a new chapter, it was the end it seemed,

No one expected him to be raised from the dead on the day of three,

He visited those who loved him at the point where their sorrow maximally seethed,

When they saw the Savior alive, they could barely believe what their eyes had seen,

When all seems lost, and there is nowhere to turn,

We can look to Jesus and ask what we have learned?

Have we learned to love, to forgive, to redeem?

Or are we stuck in our old ways like the Jews who screamed?

They screamed for crucifixion,

They achieved their vision,

Clouded by pomp, condemnation, and hate,

We must remove ourselves from this before it's too late

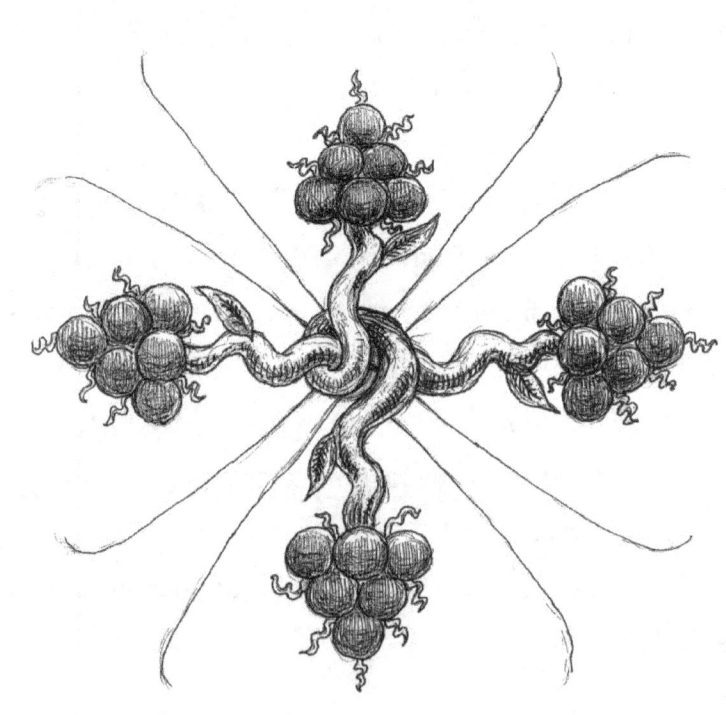

I've attempted suicide more than once, and I've had numerous occasions where I took massive amounts of drugs not necessarily wanting to die, but also not caring if I lived. One such night crept close and clutched me in its jaw as a snake creeps upon an unassuming rabbit. I had just moved from Florida to Oklahoma after embarrassing my family at a Christmas party. I packed all my belongings in my car and traveled the country looking for something, I didn't know what, and by chance (so I thought) I decided to stop in Oklahoma City on New Year's eve to visit an old High School friend from my Georgia days.

Accustomed to perusing tinder incessantly on my eternal mission to find a solution outside of myself, I matched with a supremely beautiful woman my second day drinking and doing drugs all day and sleeping in my car at night. We went on a date the next day, and something special happened. I met the girl I had always dreamed of, and although she knew I was homeless she somehow saw past that and helped me out where she could. She had her life together, and let me stay at her house occasionally, but didn't want to upset her landlords (parents) so I couldn't stay more than 3 days out of the week. Quite the "come up", met the girl my spirit had been pleading for, and got to take a shower a couple times a week. Not bad.

One of the nights I was in my car I was incredibly upset, and so I decided to take 35-40 Benadryl pills (the drug I primarily abused during my last days in Florida). I had avoided taking any Benadryl since I had moved to Oklahoma 2-3 months earlier, so I had no tolerance; I also took 10-15 more than I had ever before, so I knew that death was a real possibility. Not even a minute after I took them, a cop pulled into the parking lot where I sat in my car. Immediately after him an undercover car pulled up, and my heart sank. I rolled down the window and he asked me "why are you shivering son", I lied of course. Luckily it was winter and freezing out so I told him, "it's cold sir and I sleep in my car, I can't keep it running all night, because I am poor". He shined his flashlight in the back seat; my blanket and pillow stood firm and confirmed my alibi. He quickly informed me that this was a public park, and I can't park here overnight, so I would have to move my vehicle to a store parking lot. Overall, he was quite kind to me, and seemed understanding of my situation. Looking back, it would have been much safer had they seen through my fib.

As soon as they pulled off, the drugs set in. The playground I was in front of was in my girlfriend's neighborhood, less than a quarter mile away. My plan was to make it to her house and sleep in her driveway. The normal trip never did occur, immediately I became delirious, confused about where I was or what I was doing; and then: blackness.

I came to about 3 hours later with a dead phone, driving on the wrong side of the road in front of the courthouse. I remember thinking to myself that I should pull over and ask for help at a Waffle House, but when I tried to practice what I would say I found myself unable to form coherent sentences. I blacked out again.

I come back to reality 2 more times in various parts of town, blacking out after each return to consciousness. The last time I came to, I was on a dirt road, in a corn field. Panic struck as I had no idea where I was, it was 1 O'clock am, I had taken the drugs nearly 6 hours prior. Normally, when I would trip on Benadryl the routine would be I would have a conversation with someone for seemingly hours, suddenly realize they weren't there and that I wasn't talking (it was all in my head), a sense of impending doom would seep into the recesses of my limited consciousness, then I would drift off again to my imagination. This time, however, I was at the point where the drugs normally would wear off and had not had any such experiences (that I remembered I might add). Suddenly I noticed someone sitting in my passenger seat. This figure had a dark hood on, and I could not see their face, and to this day I can't remember what their voice sounded like. I looked for a few seconds, then they looked at me, they started with a whisper at first but their voice slowly grew to a scream, "faster... Faster.... FASTER... FASTER FASTER FASTER!"

My attention snapped back to the road when I felt movement from my back tire, the thing next to me vanished, and my car was fishtailing (swaying in the back). I looked at my speedometer, my speed had increased from 10 mph to 75 mph. I tried to correct the wheel 3-4 times, each time the car swayed more in the opposite direction. I felt fully sober at this point, adrenaline I suppose, and so I took my foot off the gas and thankfully had the presence of mind to not hit the break. At my last attempt at course correction my car swayed to the point where I could see the front of the road out of my passenger window. My whole life flashed before my eyes, but not my past, rather the potential life I was about to lose the opportunity to experience, a home, children, accomplishments, purpose. Suddenly I spun the wheel all the way to the left and then slightly to the right, and the car faced forward once more. I dealt with more small wobbles as the car slowed back down to 15, and I followed the gravel and dirt road until it led to a paved road. But here's the kicker: it didn't really feel like I was the one who straightened out the car, it felt like someone else jumped into my body and did it for me. Each turn I made ended up being the right one and I made it back to my girlfriend's house in 30 or so minutes without having to make any U Turns or course corrections, even though I didn't know my way around the city or have GPS. When I got to her house, I walked in, laid down next to her, and prayed for the first time in years, "God, please let me wake up, don't let me die in my sleep."

When I woke up the next morning I had the same thoughts that remain with me to this day, nearly 6 years later. That "thing" in the passenger seat could have been explained by drug psychosis, but I knew in my heart it was something spiritual, and not the good kind of spirit. What made this thought take hold even more was the fact that my chances of not flipping my car and perishing with my car at a 90-degree angle were cosmically small. Not to mention the fact that I knew in my heart, down to my very bones, that I myself did not make that car straighten out.

That very night was the reason I began to believe that we are not alone, and I'm not talking about aliens. I didn't turn to my creator for help with my everyday struggles, but I became aware that there are good spiritual powers, and bad. I have only attempted to tell this story to one person, perhaps two, and never finished. I suppose it's quite long and far-fetched, and I feared what other people would think; I myself would not believe it if it had not happened to me, if I hadn't experienced it. I suppose I feel comfortable putting it in this book for a few reasons: this book is about how I came out of the shadows and into the light and this was the start of it, you read this far by choice I'm not roping you in to listen to me speak for twenty minutes, and perhaps the experience will serve to entertain or help someone identify with it. The night I realized God existed, the beginning of the end of a chapter.

When Lucifer Became Satan

The beast in the deep glaring from the abyss,

Is a crease in the seam of the pairing of ignorance and bliss,

A kiss?

Consider it a miss,

The vein would have felt much better,

But then the silver cord would be severed,

The brain unshackled reveals,

The true shame of the master unveiled,

Tell me now, what's after?

Do you yearn for laughter?

Now tell me from whom?

The one who wants you to suffer all the way to the tomb?

Or God who plans paradise for you as you're stitched in the womb,

Gloom, doom,

Seemingly as if only sorrow is set to loom,

It's too bad we're never taught how hard life is for the flower before

and after it blooms,

But even the cyst would have to admit there's a void in its ploy,

All we'd have to do is open our eyes,

Is it really clever to hide truth in lies?

Succumb to, or run to,

Is it this world or the creator who funds you?

Spread love,

Or spread blood,

If you think there is anything close to a middle ground,

Then it's time you hit your knees and plead to be found,

You've never committed rape? Of course, you would never,

But you decide to stay in your lane? How is that any better?

To see evil and ignore its existence,

Is to bleed pitiful and sign your permission,

Stand and spread your wings, God gave you free will,

Your actions can cripple kings, their evil made nil,

Who is your employer, who governs what you do?

Do you worship the destroyer, without any clue?

Compete, deplete,

Success is undressed,

Have you climbed the pyramid?

Who have you stepped upon?

Which virtue did you win with?

Are you sure you weren't wrong?

Praise be to God that the more victories the enemy claims,

The further he marches toward his twisted fate,

He may be able to eternally twist the narrative,

He only does this because he knows the end and he's scared of it,

His light is darkness visible,

For his fight is less than pitiful,

A worm would be insulted to be called the Morning Star,

His turn to be exalted for his fall is in mourning a scar,

He was our Fathers' once proudest creation,

When man was created, Lucifer became Satan,

I like to imagine what he must have said, what thoughts went through his mind,

His ego was threatened with death and so he betrayed each of our kind,

Perhaps that's why I used to think I saw him in the mirror,

The parts of him in me have never revealed themselves clearer,

The one who is said to bring sublime wisdom,

Is turning our very world into a slime kingdom,

I happily await the day he suffers his time fiendom,

What can I do? Other than happily await our promised conclusion?

I suppose I can follow you and help lead our brothers from confusion,

And Phosphorus, since I know you're fuming,

I know it's preposterous, but I hope your guilt is consuming,

Because the one I follow tells me to love my foe,

So, no matter the sorrow, I'll visit where you can never go,

I give you my compassion, and pray that you change,

So I can spread Jesus' fashion, even if it seems strange,

Although our goals are clashing it won't close the curtain on stage

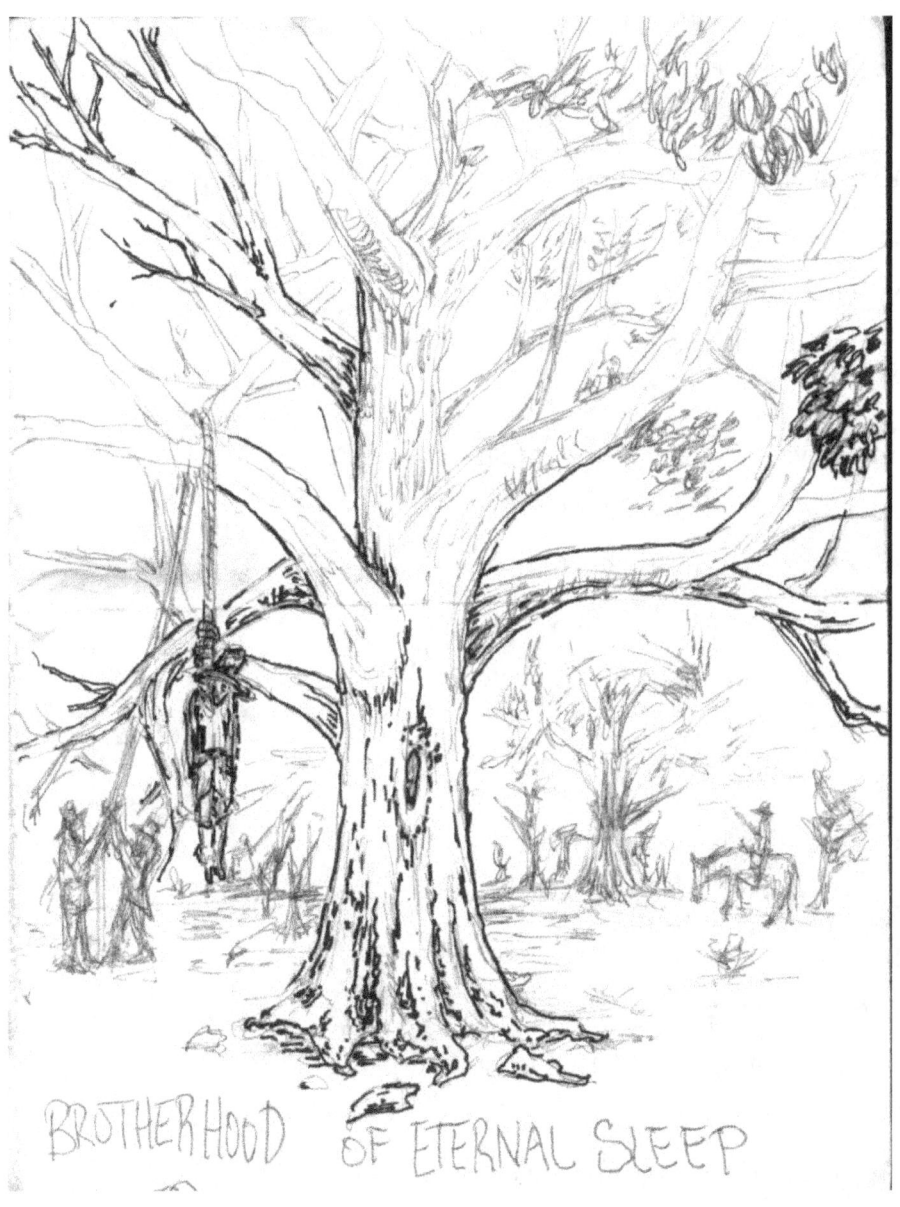

Love thy Enemy

Will these demons ever leave?
Will my mental state ever stabilize?
Is there any lasting reprieve?
Or am I destined to be terrorized?

The constant push and pull,
Being torn limb from limb,
Will my mind ever be able,
To not succumb to every whim?

Impulsive, delusional, full of fear,
Compulsive, with ritual, of evil near,
Many men have preached of escape,
But have they hated all they see?
Only then can life teem with hate,
Of the powers always at be,

This war that has been waged,
Since before time was recorded,
Has kept many ignorant souls caged,
And too many good souls aborted,
What sort of battle is more difficult,
That one that no one knows of?
My generation sees religion as a cult,

And struggle to even believe in love,

Divorce rates, and murder rates,

At the highest any man can remember,

Garbage heaps full of full plates,

While elsewhere children are dismembered,

The priorities, of this society,

Are unmistakable, truly one of a kind,

If you saw the adversary,

Then you'd see the truth of the mind,

In order to come close,

One must admit of themselves they are nothing,

And that vanity can only boast,

Self-importance and self-inflicted eternal suffering,

Resistance to change,

Keeps the mind deranged,

And allows shackles to remain,

Do you want to break free?

To see yourself in me?

And love your enemy?

My Name is Greed

Insanity is a trait I broadcast,

As vanity innate in the outcast,

Go on and tell me I'm a completely derailed genius,

To see his filthy entrails against my spirits cleanness,

Do you see this?

The portal through which we are thrust,

Asking if I'm immortal, this is my crutch,

I know I'm not, says the liar,

I enjoy walking through shots fired,

Put a pistol to my skull, to bring me out of,

The bristle of this lull, back to true love,

A fool? Who me?

No, I simply use my lack of sanity,

To bleed everything else out of society,

In the cauldron that seethes with constant calamity,

Pleased to meet you, my name is Greed,

Please, you think I can't bring you to your knees?

I am one of the few who can; yes, indeed!

Flesh May Burn

Flesh may burn, but bones don't bleed,

Demons converge, on my dreams they feed,

I need your sympathy but don't pity me,

This is simply a show of how one sows what he reaps,

In the bare reaches of the depth of despair,

The man I once lost, he resides in there,

A man within,

A man victim to sin,

His own desires,

Lead to those eternal fires,

A smile across the lips of a lover,

Released from the devils' guile, no longer undercover,

Once upon a time on that lonely road,

Sunlight transpires ever releasing a lonesome coat,

I wanted more but I'm near less,

Call me as my friends do, that is, fearless,

I claim to crave a revolution, but my actions show a desire for revelation,

I must be saved from confusion otherwise this can be my suicides declaration

Travis Johnston

Hypnotized by the Dream

I stand mystified by the trauma ties,

That leaves us stuck in our feeble cries,

Clear to see the tables turn on our demise,

Damaged eyes? That hardly describes,

The mist that leaves you and I trusting in lies,

Simple? Surely you don't think this is so,

I know in the end we reap what we sow,

Hypnotized by the dream,

That in which we reside it seems,

The labor of the wicked is this,

The common man labeled as sickened by bliss,

Statistical is the wicked one's pull,

Put this into your database:

It's too commonplace that the only commonality,

In the human race is that we're all full of hate,

That's misplaced and tends to gravitate to our neighbors face,

What a true disgrace,

It makes me irate with anger,

It's our beauty innate that's in danger,

But there is salvation lying outside of the grasp of rules of nations,

They curse us or they fear our collaboration or worse, the near hour
of their damnation,

United we stand? Divided we fall?

Perhaps we've been defeated after all

What would life be like for us as individuals if there were no light in the world? If the sun never shined, or if we were stuck in a perpetual solar eclipse? For starters our human eyes would not be suited for it, we would run into walls, stumble, and fall frequently. We would be dependent on external powers to see even our hand in front of our face, such as flashlights, phones, glow sticks, something that emits some kind of light. You wouldn't be able to put on your makeup right or fix your hair, because you wouldn't be able to see your reflection in the mirror.

This is what it is like to live in the shadows. Our human minds aren't suited for it. We blame ourselves, which makes sense since we are seemingly placed in the dark by our own actions, led by our own thoughts and emotions. When living in the shadows one desperately searches for anything that emits light or power, vices such as drugs, sex, and love of money do the trick better than absolutely nothing. We do things we don't want to do and feel too weak to do the things that we want. We live in fear and thus feel like we know no love, certainly not love for the self. And although we see our physical self clearly in the mirror, we can't look ourselves in the eyes, because we lie, steal, cheat; it's become more and more a part of our nature as we grow accustomed to living in the dark, shut off from the sunlight of the spirit. Although it has *become* a part of our nature, this doesn't mean that's what our hearts or minds, our soul if you will, wants. The person we want to be doesn't line up with our actions, and we all know that the road to hell is paved with good intentions.

Mental illness and addiction isn't as rare as some would like to believe, I think they are just extreme reactions to our soul's rejecting this world, we're homesick; it's the human condition. We all suffer from the human condition; many philosophies and ways of life have been created to try to overcome this very thing. Buddhism is a good example. I think it is no coincidence that seemingly everyone who has turned their life around proudly announces that it was because they found something greater than themselves. It makes sense does it not? The human condition is created because this world breeds suffering, so how do we overcome the world? Only by something greater than this world. The universe is greater than this world, the creator is greater than the creation, and nearly a third of the world's population believes that the Son of God was sent here for the very purpose of conquering this world.

So, when you're ready, step out of the shadows. Take a chance; best case scenario you experience the light of day for maybe the first time ever, worst case? Well, can it get much worse? Face it, many of us live our worst-case scenario mentally and spiritually every day. Take the leap, step from bridge to shore, join in union with the creator. Creation was never meant to survive separate from its creator.

The Schism

The schism that creates the division, the wall between dark and light,

Is our prism that is life's vision; a journey to embark, quite the sight,

Our existence is stitched upon such a fine line,

Blood glistens as we draw nearer to salvation of our minds eye,

What once helped us trudge along and avoid fatal plight,

Has now swelled in sludge and created a void dark as night,

Brick by brick the dooms been built,

Tick by tick comes the gloom, sins guilt,

Truth will be revealed; the sunlight will come to pass,

But my fate is sealed, for your sight is never to last,

In a dream I am blessed and cursed with the presence of your soul,

I awake and scream hurting worse for your absence takes its toll,

I chose the drug over one true love,

The grave I dug left me on my back looking above,

It was in that trance I lay staring at a starlit night,

My second chance coming with surrender to the fight,

I suppose the tone of my life's adventure as it currently stands,

Is the flesh and bone of the man I am,

Crumbling for all of eternity just like times sand

What I Resemble

Seduce, reduce, keep up the ruse,

There's nothing I wouldn't do,

To deceive you,

And pass fake proof,

As the truth,

While inside my mind,

I know you're not mine,

Because the man you think I am is a figment created from fragments

of my past,

The only thing for certain is that this illusion I create surely won't

last,

So at night, in a sweat, I tremble,

Living in fright of what I resemble,

That's the trouble,

The life I live,

Is one that's double,

So my life I give,

To futures rubble

Misery

Obsessed, caressed, I shelter the pest,

Not to cause distress for I know he does his best,

To turn my genius mind into an absolute and utter mess,

I can't seem to get these thoughts out of my head,

Knowing full well my disease wants nothing but my death,

A voice in my head, oh how it sounds like me,

Every lie has been said, driving me to self-pity,

Have I had enough? I want the answer to be yes,

These mental gymnastics leave me gasping for a breath,

When every thought my mind creates is about new ways to use,

I can't help but wonder if abstinence is the worse form of abuse,

Seeds have been planted but they haven't grown,

Indeed, they're supplanted and I'm the last to know,

Or perhaps I saluted as the first,

It's all convoluted, it leaks into a verse,

I seem to hear demons converse,

Misery what they need to quench the thirst

Bones Don't Bleed

Despair in the air, oh how time flies,

It matches smiles, it matches cries,

The bodies land in a pile, a lake of rage hidden behind blue eyes,

It matches guile, it matches some long sought after group demise,

A story told by a feeble hand,

A sought after cure in evils land,

Transcending or descending, is the choice even mine?

My talents been lost it seems to the sands of time,

A wicked cure, a sickened blur,

All the while I'm all but sure,

Pain has reached its limit and slowly recedes,

Flesh may burn but bones don't bleed

Never Above

I love you; I'll hug you, and I'll show you the way,

But my feet must show you regardless of what I say,

Without hard work I torture myself trying to play,

So although so few options remain I'll continue to pray,

Because if I'm not leading with action then what's the use?

If my mouth is out of sync with my hands then I'm outside of truth,

13 inches is the journey from a man's nose to his heart,

I couldn't see past my nose, seeing you is a start,

When I was drenched in fire,

I couldn't be quenched as the liar,

It's a web as complex as the number zero, so large I cannot describe,

Infinity is really miniscule, all that we're taught is a lie,

Hence our souls send the body on a quest to quickly die,

Although we're all born to do this in between we ought to fly,

I've searched for love in the bottom of a glass,

Deluding my mind to thinking any feeling will last,

When really each feeling is fleeting just like my heart as its beating,

But even that sound is buried by my fears and their bleating,

And my thoughts and their screeching,

Pain covers blasphemed truth since I feel most alive when I'm bleeding,

The escape?

There is none from fate,

Which we know, it's simply innate,

That's the rub; the answer must be acceptance and love,

Once I saw that providence prevails, I understood God is within,

never above

First impressions are often the worst impressions, at least, in my experiences. My first impressions on alcohol and its effects on me were wrong, my first impression on Methamphetamine was most assuredly way off, I can think of countless relationships that developed in a way that I never expected. How many friends do I have that I felt negatively towards in our first interaction? Was this not due to countless forms of insecurity, fear, prejudices, and the like. How many adversaries did I once think were my friends? Was this not due to codependency, loneliness, fear, lack of self-love, and countless other unhealthy character traits?

For the vast majority of my life, I have lived in the shadow of self-deceit, hallmarked by the omission of the facts. I learned, not much different from a lot of men and women, from a young age to suppress my true feelings and not ask for help. Trapped in a cycle of not being honest with others and trying to brave the storm alone creates the perfect potion for not having the capacity to be honest with oneself. I grew into the habit of shutting my mind against looking at how wrong my judgments were, and how blessed I am that my expectations are rarely met. Not to mention, who has the right to judge? Many of the actions, thoughts, and feelings that I have judged my fellows for I have been guilty of myself. So I find that when I judge others, I really pass judgment on myself; and besides, does it ever produce good feelings or thoughts when our instinct is to immediately judge those around us?

I believe one of the benefits of writing this excerpt for publication is that most humans don't realize when they are living in fear or insecurity. Those of us who are driven by fears are constantly let down by expectations, angered by assumptions we make about what others actions mean or what they are thinking, and miss out on countless relationships and opportunities that could change the course of our very lives. I read a book, at the beginning of my journey, that really helped me out. The four agreements, the topic of the book, are as follows: always be impeccable with your word, don't make assumptions, don't take anything personally, and always do your best.

I didn't immediately incorporate all of these into my life, but the words immediately registered with me. What is right and what is wrong has been written in laws throughout all of human history, but more importantly, it's written in our hearts. Our word is our bond, and words have the power to destroy or to transform. Making assumptions prevents us from asking questions, and indicates quite a high level of arrogance which usually goes unnoticed by the assumer. We live in a world disconnected, a spiritual existence ruled by material possessions, so to take personally someone else's sick ways is to take on their sickness; we have enough sickness of our own, we don't need to make our fellows disease our own. Finally, our best fluctuates wildly day to day, but if you stick to your best each day regrets cease to exist as long as we realize that there isn't failure other than quitting but rather there are learning experiences.

I prefer to write poetry, I really do. Everything else in this book is my experiences, opinions, and my truth. Art is interpreted on a personal level for each person who enjoys it, and thus more beautiful in my opinion; but there is some merit in adding some philosophy between the beauty, just in case anyone desires to understand why the poet writes what he or she does. So bear with me, if you will, or you can just skip all this bullshit and go to the art. You won't hurt my feelings.

Liars Fire

Even drenched in fire,

I cannot be quenched as the liar,

Incapable of the truth, I don't mean to lie,

But if I don't to you how can I deceive my mind,

How can I motivate my legs to go get a victory,

When I'm insane and seek out the death of me?

I can no longer deny what I hear or see,

But now I can't even trust if I'm still living in reality,

That of which is stitched along a seam,

Do you trust your eyes enough to believe what you see?

Oh pity, that bottomless pit of morose,

No matter the city I hold my shadow self ever close,

To no one's surprise I lost it all, except this pen,

I wrote my soul's desire once, can I do it again?

Or is it to Hell that my talent was sent?

I wouldn't break if I learned how to bend,

But now this seems like the end,

The curtain indeed,

Demons have been sent,

On my dreams they feed,

I desperately want to be freed,

But I must ask: what's the use?

You successfully planted a seed,

But it didn't survive the abuse

Eternal Shame

There's anger, there's danger, you already know,

Demons unseen taunt me wherever I go,

They use my emotions against me; they're all in a throw,

In the end the lesson is that we reap what we sow,

The fragments of my past have left my bones withering within,

The dogma of the expired soul is that his patience was worn thin,

Pain, we're the same,

For we both make our host quite insane

And it is his eternal shame,

That he is the origin from which we came

Nothing of Your View

I run from you, I near my escape,

My soul is blue, in my dream you await,

Perhaps this is what they call fate,

A man destined to suffer in your losses wake,

Of course it was my fault, truly so,

Peace runs as it is sought, this I know,

I seem to have forgotten nothing of your view,

It is etched into my mind, the memory of you,

I can't help but feel weak and pathetic,

I weep at dreams that seem prophetic,

I close my eyes and drift away,

In my dreams you visit but never stay,

Alas it's the lass,

That curses my past,

Creating the bellow, that echoes,

The one heard by my fellows,

So this is my curse,

I can imagine no pain worse,

I now must traverse a fiend's life,

Where we converse in a dream at night

Providence Prevails

This pain in my chest has morphed to pain in my head,

My heart can't seem to find any solace or rest,

I look in the mirror, and what do I see?

A jagged reflection glaring back at me,

A life full of rejection and inadequacy,

I starved so many of water so they could not grow,

Now I know my debt, it's my soul that I owe,

Pitter patter, the rain falls,

Splitter splatter, blood on the walls,

And who could be responsible for it all?

I hit my knees and plead with God,

Almighty please stop catching me as I fall,

Now I hear all the demons applaud,

My prayer is answered to no avail,

So, it turns out in the end,

I have to admit that Providence will prevail,

With angels' heaven sent

Polluted

Deluded, polluted, I'm surrounded by mist,
The fogs in my mind as I grow ever more sick,
And the blood has become thick,

But what am I to do?
I grow more confused,
By what I feel
As I lay next to you,

The time bomb's been defused,
By the sweat that pours,
For I am truly profuse,
Due to your smile of course,

I seem to be truly destined for implosion,
Due to this cancer and this body it grows in,
So many towels have been thrown in,

But not quite mine,
I know the enemies that persist,
Are from my own mind,
When I question if I exist,
It's simply more questions I find

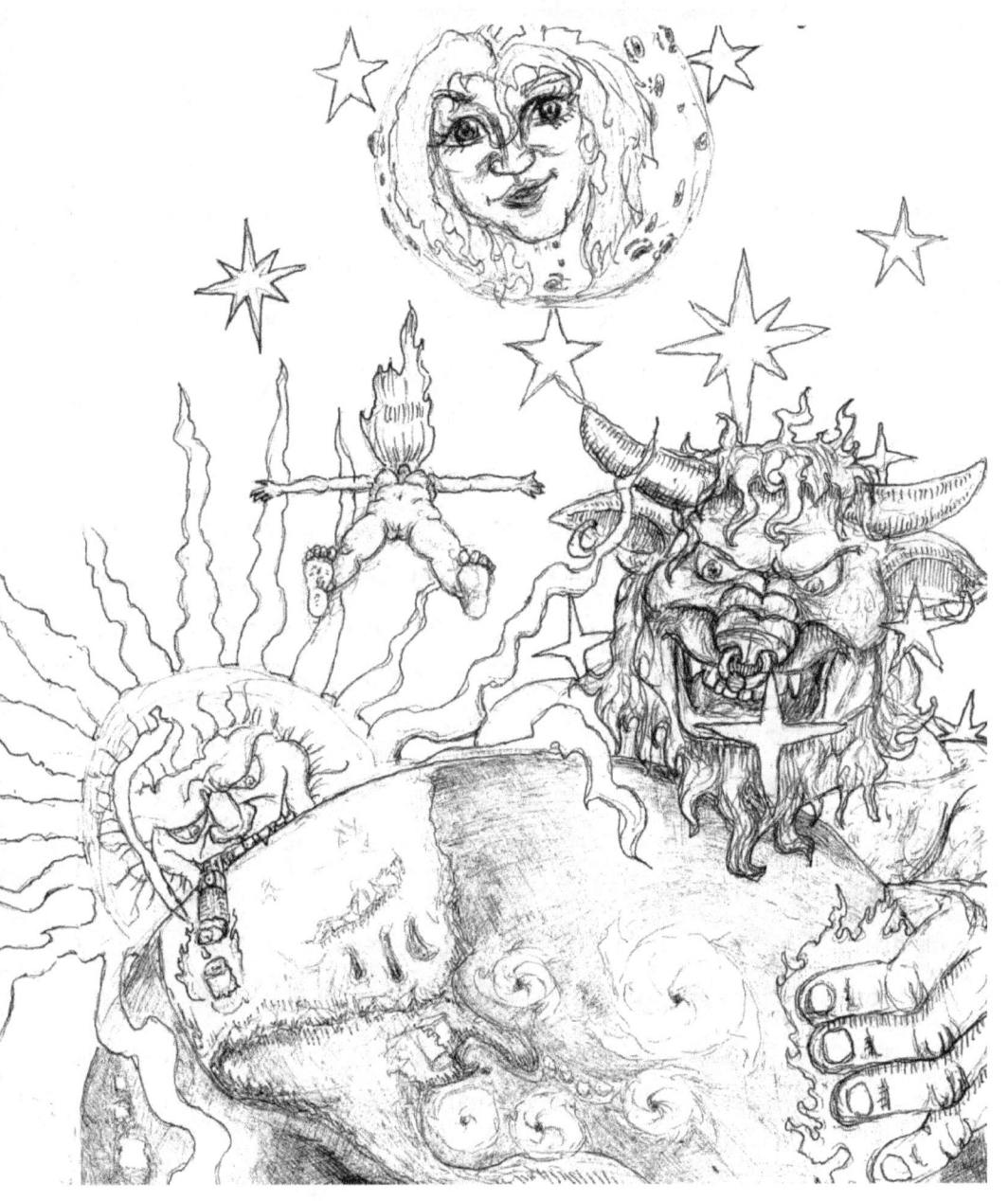

It's taken my whole life but it finally dawned on me, what I've been told for over a decade. What other people think of me is none of my business. I realize now that I also really shouldn't want it to be. Here on Earth we will discover amazing friendships, passionate loves, bitter adversaries; sometimes the friendships will become loves, the loves adversaries, and the adversaries friends. I have come to understand that the end result of these relationships were always meant to be and the original connection was a misjudgment. In the end other people will show the nature of their tether to you, and it's rarely in our control and nearly never under our full control.

I've lived my whole life constantly worried about the ever-shifting landscape of my fellow man's opinion of me, while blotting out the awareness that there is one entity who never changes its mind, or changes who it is. I call it a He. He's God, Creator, an all knowing presence.

I'm joyful that I've been permitted to realize the importance of shifting my intention to pleasing the one who sees all from pleasing the fickle minds of human beings. Of course I want to make my family proud, and my friends who have become family. As for everyone else? Fuck em. I don't say that aggressively, rather as a matter of fact. People, for the most part, will always judge. I'm not interested in their judgment; they usually judge by the standard of what they can see. God judges by what is seen and what we cannot see, for he sees what is done in the dark.

To be honest, it's a huge relief. The God I believe in makes it supremely clear how He is pleased: by showing the same kindness and love to my friends and enemies, the same kindness and love He showed me even when I was his enemy. His nature isn't constantly shifting like some people, His words remain forever true, He cannot lie, and His judgment is free of all our sick thoughts. I have much less to worry about when I try to please God and am not faced with constantly disappointing someone while trying to please another. God is the better way, the best way!

Reflection

I lay in the cold, quite profuse,

From the pain of frequent abuse,

As I lay in the rain on the roof,

I promised I wouldn't lie to you, so I present myself as I am,

I look in the mirror and it's true I gaze at a strange man,

And walk around aimlessly in a daze in a strange land,

A prophecy leaves me,

Looking at the heavens as I bleed,

My chest heaves as I struggle to breathe,

But don't pity me, please,

It was what I sowed that I now reap,

A multitude of seeds planted,

With profits seized I've been supplanted,

I hate to rant but also hate to sit in silence,

So instead I speak or I act in violence,

And I can't cry or smile,

Or understand Satan's guile as a tyrant,

I'm hoping that there must be a reset,

For I can't survive with this preset,

I've arrived at the conclusion, at last, that I must be reborn,

For I can't survive the link between my heart and mind being torn,

So where can I turn?
There is one thing I've learned,
No matter how far I've searched,
I've found that everything I've ever needed resides within,
Returning to the mirror,
I smile at myself, and ask my reflection: where have you been?

Abyss Above

With breath heavy and blood soaking through my hair,

I ask death why he won't let me come to that place over there,

The here-after has always called my name,

What I'm after has left me dumb, blind, and lame,

Forever bound to the thought of a lost flame,

With a quivering voice,

I want to return to that, from which I came,

I've been robbed of choice,

So instead I gaze at the abyss above,

While all else worry about what's below,

In all the wrong places I've looked for love,

I've learned we all reap what we sow,

It doesn't matter which way we go,

What turns we choose to make,

At least now I finally know,

I'd rather give than be one to take

The Puppeteer

The Puppeteer,

Holds me dear,

Perhaps this is why I sense maleficence,

Forever near,

Maleficence or magnificence,

Can they ever coexist?

Perhaps all that makes sense is my ability to persist,

To stare down the massive emptiness of the abyss,

Darkness that light cannot even pervade,

The light cannot pierce the dark,

How easily can the blackness persuade,

On this journey that we choose to embark,

We see the grim reaper presented in suede,

A knock on my door, but it's your house he invades,

I came across him often, you can say, we're friends today,

A daze I cannot seem to escape,

From outside it looks like a haze,

On which my friend death satiates,

Pitter patter,

The nimble mouse sneaks around,

Splitter splatter,

Blood covering the house we found,

Solution? I pollute it,

My thoughts conquer my heart,

You could say that I suit it,

I've been wrangled and torn apart

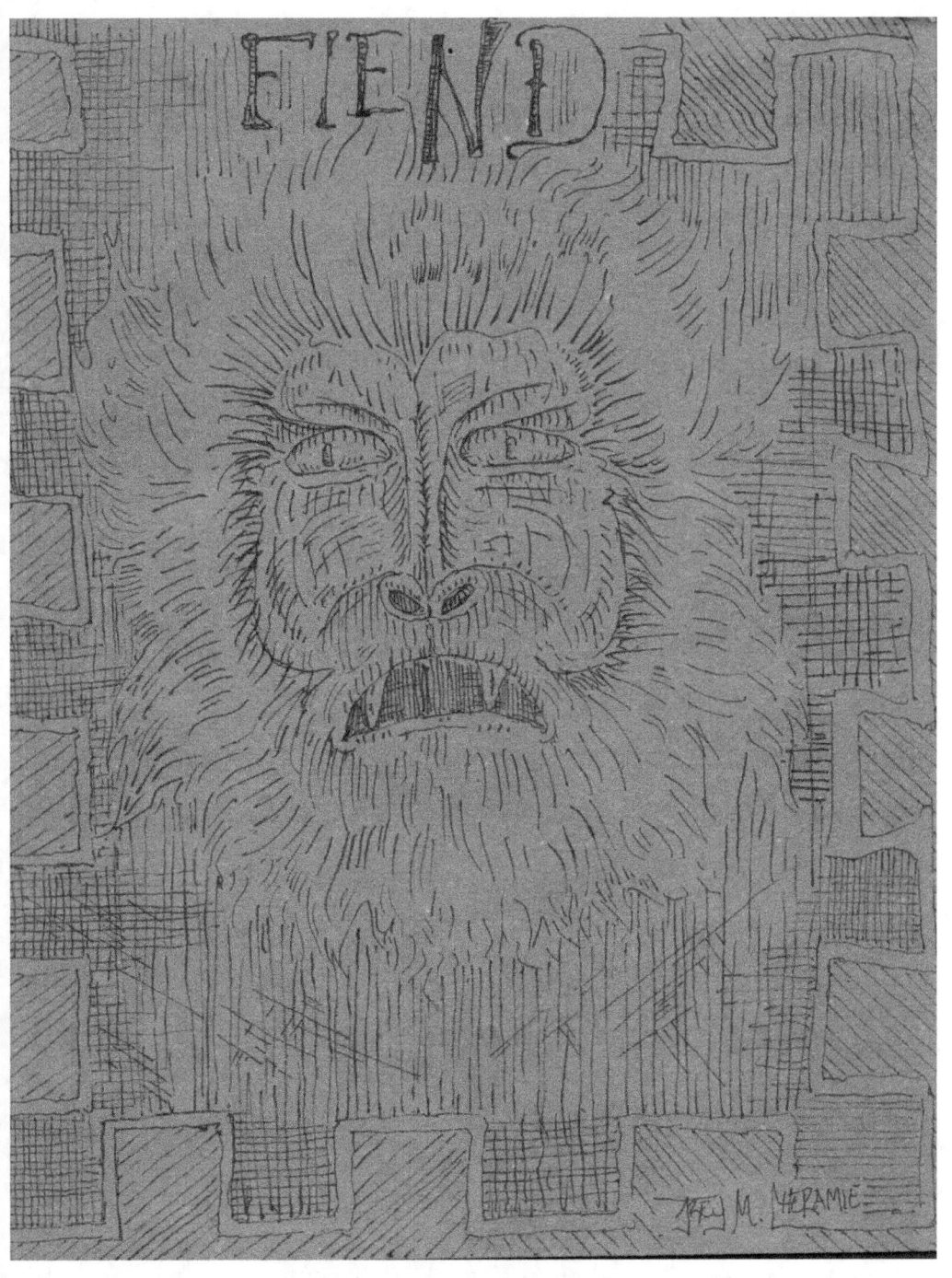

Divine Creation

A sample is ample evidence to describe,

The sea of pain hidden behind green eyes,

Guilt ridden by the weight of his crimes,

Pain screeching from the passage of time,

Faces pass, some seem as if they are meant to last,

While some reappear as he has night terrors linked to his past,

Alas it's the lass,

She curses his past,

Creating the bellows,

Heard by his fellows,

Confusion from the suture of reality stitched along a seam,

Present and past linked in a chemical romance that seethes,

He cannot find any escape from this combination it seems,

As he's sowing seeds hoping they'll turn into future trees,

That will eventually bear fruit that he can eat,

That may be able to sustain his spirit and meet all its needs,

Yet the problem is that he is running from what he cannot escape,

That thing is him, with a hunger for sorrow that will never satiate,

Out on the ocean there is not a single witness,

To view the commotion he creates in an effort to feel less,

Numb, he latches on to the simple fact that he is still young,

As he ages, he can no longer cope with all that he's done,

A need for symmetry is simply innate in our nature,

He fiends for simplicity but fate seems to be his savior,

What he questions now he will believe easily much later,

This happens naturally as divine creation bleeds onto paper

The Tempter

Was it the tempter who sent her, all that time ago,

We met and then I left her, now regret is all I know,

A sample is ample evidence to describe,

The sea of pain hidden behind ocean blue eyes,

Guilt ridden by the weight of my crimes,

Undeserving of the relief of tears, I can't cry,

Presumptuous, my demons love this, for I cannot ascend,

To the pits of hell I traverse, it is here I descend,

At least now I can write a verse, on paper, from pen,

But how could it be worse? For this began with an end,

Some things I'll never get back for to heaven they're sent,

I used to think I wouldn't break if I learned how to bend,

I can see this is erroneous now, if I use common sense,

Forget past and future, now I'm alone, present tense,

Can I have time to atone in the next life and be heaven sent?

I suppose I could don the label schemer. I have always been one to have a plan, and a backup plan, and a backup plan to the backup plan. In many of the 12 step programs a common question when one makes it back from a relapse is 'have you run out of ideas/plans yet?'. This is such a common question because most people who suffer with an addiction really have to get to the point where any idea that comes out of our own noggin has to be not only held up to the light to determine its true nature but has to be entirely thrown out on the assumption that the idea is in fact not a good one.

I'm sure addicts are kept company by many 'regular' people in the prison of our own minds. More than just addicts are enslaved to their own thoughts, which breed worry, resentment, anxious tendencies, and the like. There have been many books written with the sole purpose of emphasizing how important it is to not live in the past or fret on the future (The Power of Now comes to mind). Constant thought of oneself whether it be about the past, future, or even present comes with plenty of negative emotions and negative thought patterns. 12 step fellowships preach that in order to be released from slavery, we have to think of others first. It makes sense when we examine where our problems come from; they are more often than not of our own design and doing.

I know, in my case, that being wrapped up with myself incessantly has led me to become arrogant, self-pitying, close minded, deceitful, afraid, etc. Only recently did it creep into my mind that I'm not the only person who suffers from this type of bondage, and it's not only my fellow addict either. This realization has made it much easier to be tolerant and nonjudgmental of others. After all, how dare I judge another person for something I myself have been guilty of? How dare I not tolerate behaviors and words that I myself have experienced tolerance for?

Awake

I bare my teeth out slow,

The same above as below,

It's do or die,

Crash or fly,

I'm done living a lie,

So here's a last goodbye,

It's a goodbye letter written to my demons,

They obsess on my deeds smitten with feeding,

Back when all my words had no meaning,

But now it's through and freedoms been won,

The sky is blue and I feel the warmth of the sun,

To be awake, finally to the truth we've been seeking all around,

Demons shake; they fear those who woke to the feeding sound,

Strength through sublime deception,

God's soldiers shine with perfection,

It's time for life to finally take a new direction,

Where we can look straight ahead at our reflection,

Perplexed

I'm perplexed,

Perhaps vexed,

It's been like this so long,

As if I've lost my way,

Of writing a new song,

This is the price I had to pay,

For choosing to live wrong,

It's like it's in my head,

But won't come out,

As if my spirits dead,

Blood spurting from a spout,

And everything I've read,

I simply want to shout,

Rather I keep it in,

Although I have no doubt,

I will succumb to sin,

The reality check,

Has me vexed,

Rhythm and rhyme,

Lost to sands of time,

Am I even alive?

What a query,

The fear in me,

I'll let it out once more,

I feel death near to me,

I feel it in my core,

And I want to soar,

But I'm weighed down,

A problem once more?

With no smile, I frown,

Yes, I've lost my way,

What more is there left to say?

Perhaps I'll be alright,

Once I surrender, today,

I will finally win the fight

Villain

I'm timid, I shake,

It seems,

I have lost my way,

So by instinct I turn my eyes to the sky,

I do all I can to push through the lies,

As I look above I pray,

I know my creator today,

My tendency to be bitter falls away,

After all I was the sinner, who had to pay,

In some ways a beginner at this game we play,

I thought I was a winner each time she stayed,

In the end I didn't lose her, I gave her away,

Left an angel crying at the foot of our bed,

I was chasing the dragon to the gates of death,

In a sea of loneliness I surface to catch my breath,

The wave's envelope, the sea is a master beyond my grasp,

Now disheveled, I see I was a bad omen, a flag at half mast,

I took, I lied,

I was the one I despised,

I believed many lies,

All to justify my crimes,

You want news of my demise,

Lying awake each night,

Tortured by tears she cried,

But now the question remains, am I the bad guy?

A song to convey the story that plays behind these eyes,

The leader of the bad guys sang,

A tune unforgotten soaked in pain,

Formaldehyde coated, it won't decay,

So perhaps you can avoid the same mistake,

The voice is raspy, the tone isn't rushed,

The choice in the asking, the crowd hushed,

As the crooks' voice bellows,

Creeping up the spine of his fellows,

He begs his creator to tell him 'Why me'?

Not until much later can he finally see,

Not why did she ever leave me, rather,

What did she ever perceive in me, splatter,

The blood's covered all over the wall,

A tear is shed as our singers' voice falls,

Suppose it has nothing to do with perfection,

He knows rather it comes down to introspection,

Indeed we have reached the end, have arrived,

At this conclusion the villain took his own life,

Now that's a show, fitting to be shown around the globe,

Was our villain a hero in the story of his own?

That is an answer that we must leave for only God knows,

His final prayer at last revealed,

A truth we can no longer conceal,

He admitted he could no longer traverse,

A lonely and dark abysmal universe,

Where only in a dream he and his beloved could converse,

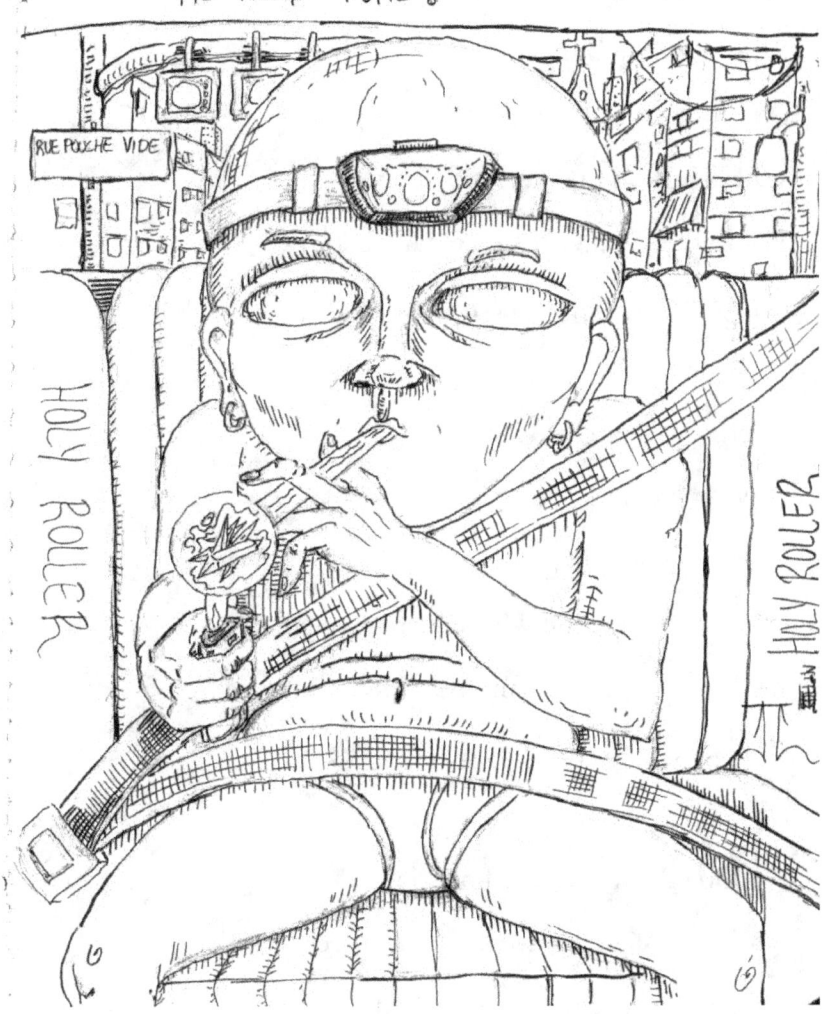

Tyrant

Sit in silence,

Steady tyrant,

With blinding blows,

Down winding slopes,

With a hilltop blanketed in snow,

The public again asks us what we know,

Our response? Feed them dope,

Overdose deaths,

Or with luck,

Comatose breaths,

Give me a machine with which to breathe,

Anything to give my mother time to bereave,

Is this the Hell that we all perceive?

We thought we escaped prison,

But it's in shackles we are conceived,

We are the cattle that they breed,

A free breath we have never breathed,

But don't worry,

It's only the whole world that's been deceived,

Oh yes, you are worthy,

You caught the hyperbole,

But don't worry, most of us sleep, just not little old me,

Now you see why I view the sheep with jealousy

Fools of Stimulation

The weight of my crimes seem to increase,

With the passage of time, the air I breathe,

But don't ask me to clear the confusion,

I'll respond with fear, why do I do this?

They oppress us with obsession,

To depress us with digression,

Look the other way,

Knowing the truth is the price I have to pay,

This abuse why I feel lonely every day,

We're fed lies from youth,

A special form of abuse,

Santa Claus is made up, a lie told to the purest,

Simply a tool of manipulation,

Creating a collision with precision, the surest,

For us fools for stimulation,

Simulate my dreams; tell me I'm enough,

I'd sell my soul just to feel the simulated touch,

So I huffed, I drank, stopped short of cold metal in my arm,

Anything for a simple release to protect my fragile ego from harm,

It drives me to depression, this oppression of the kind,

Drugs were a last resort to protect the recesses of my mind,

The upheaval and unrest of a society simply put into rhyme,

This sorrow just as sure as the passage of the sands of time,

But now I have a choice, one so few people have achieved,

A new way to use my voice, to share the ideas I've conceived,

To scream from the hilltop the reality of this world we traverse,

I use these pages as a forum where God and I converse,

My creator, how is it I will get them to see?

What more can I do, just little old me?

The sun peaks through the blind; all I needed was a sign,

One that with earnest, the good Lord decided to provide,

This ray of light has proven to me that I'm doing just fine

As someone who suffers from addiction, I have been in plenty of ambulances, and have interacted with plenty of healthcare personnel who are labeled as 'normal'. Occasionally they'll ask me why I do what I do, why I continue to use drugs even though they clearly have impacted my physical and mental health in extremely detrimental ways. Honestly, it's never an enjoyable conversation, partly because usually I've been up for days and am hallucinating badly, and partly because I myself don't even understand why I keep making the same painful mistake repeatedly.

Generally, I'll try to explain what it's like to these helpful people; what it's like to not be able to trust your own thoughts. I've relapsed many times, and only after this most recent one did I realize that I've been lying to myself for years in sobriety and in active use. I know that the solution is being honest, open minded, and willing. I am easily able to convince myself that I am checking all the boxes whenever I am not being honest about my emotions, whenever I'm not sharing my innermost thoughts with another. The emotions that get bottled up and never discussed end up getting written off, or my thoughts use them to twist the narrative and turn me into a victim. Once I'm the victim I don't have to take a look at how I was wrong in a certain situation and thus there is no room for me to grow. By not sharing my thoughts with my fellow man, I have no one to point out where I am wrong or where I need to challenge unhealthy thinking patterns.

After only a few months of staying in this state of mind a relapse is sure to come. A good illustration of what it's really like to be an addict would show a person in a constant state of debate, with themselves. I remember one of the few times I ever stole from a person. I took 40 dollars out of my ex-girlfriend's babysitting money jar (I was sober but planning to relapse), then I went to her work and handed her the money while apologizing for taking it. She was upset that I stole it but glad that I didn't choose to relapse. Later that night, I took the money out of the jar again then went and bought meth with it. She found out the next day. Let's not talk about how stupid that sounds, because it does, I know. Let's talk about how this is the perfect example of what it's like to be an addict every day when the obsession is on his back like a monkey that is choking him out. I debated with myself for hours before I took her money, then I felt ashamed and returned it, then I impulsively took it again and bought drugs. Rationalizing, justifying, debating, acting on impulse, and experiencing shame: the daily life of an addict.

My Demise

As I am buried by a lie, it's as if I'm being buried alive,

How else can I escape the passage of time?

How else can I withstand the last of my crimes?

These questions outline the fate, to which I am resigned,

Navigated a path was taken, but amnesia took hold,

I have coal all around me I mistook it as gold,

A sample is ample evidence when it comes to the tides,

I looked all around me for God when he was always inside,

I keep looking for a new partner but see you in each of their eyes,

Perhaps this curse is fitting for the ways I assured your outcries,

I continue to plead with God to give me an escape or a sign,

Rather than a signal I'm met with the uncertainty of my demise,

Memories Treachery

I must ask why I torture myself with these memories' treachery,

My minds task to venture into the murky past to get the best of me,

My past and future wrestle me,

Can I never wrest satisfaction out of this life?

At last, the suture nestles me,

Is it best for me to succumb to this strife?

It's as if spiritual bankruptcy can never be achieved,

Each time I see a glimpse of it, even more I bleed,

I don't think I'll arrive there until I no longer breathe,

But all of my being remains under siege,

As if I'm a lonely sailor, lost forever to the seas,

Alone, I must atone for the crimes that litter my past,

I avoid the ringing phone because this glitter never lasts,

Of course, it's the woman raising the flag of black mast,

There is a funeral for my soul, with the attendance of none,

Just I encouraging my soul to return from which we come,

Perhaps, me, myself, and I are really more than one,

Like the holy trinity, and the kingdom still to come,

Perhaps turning above can help the mess in my mind come undone,

I can finally turn from the darkness and feel my face bask in the sun

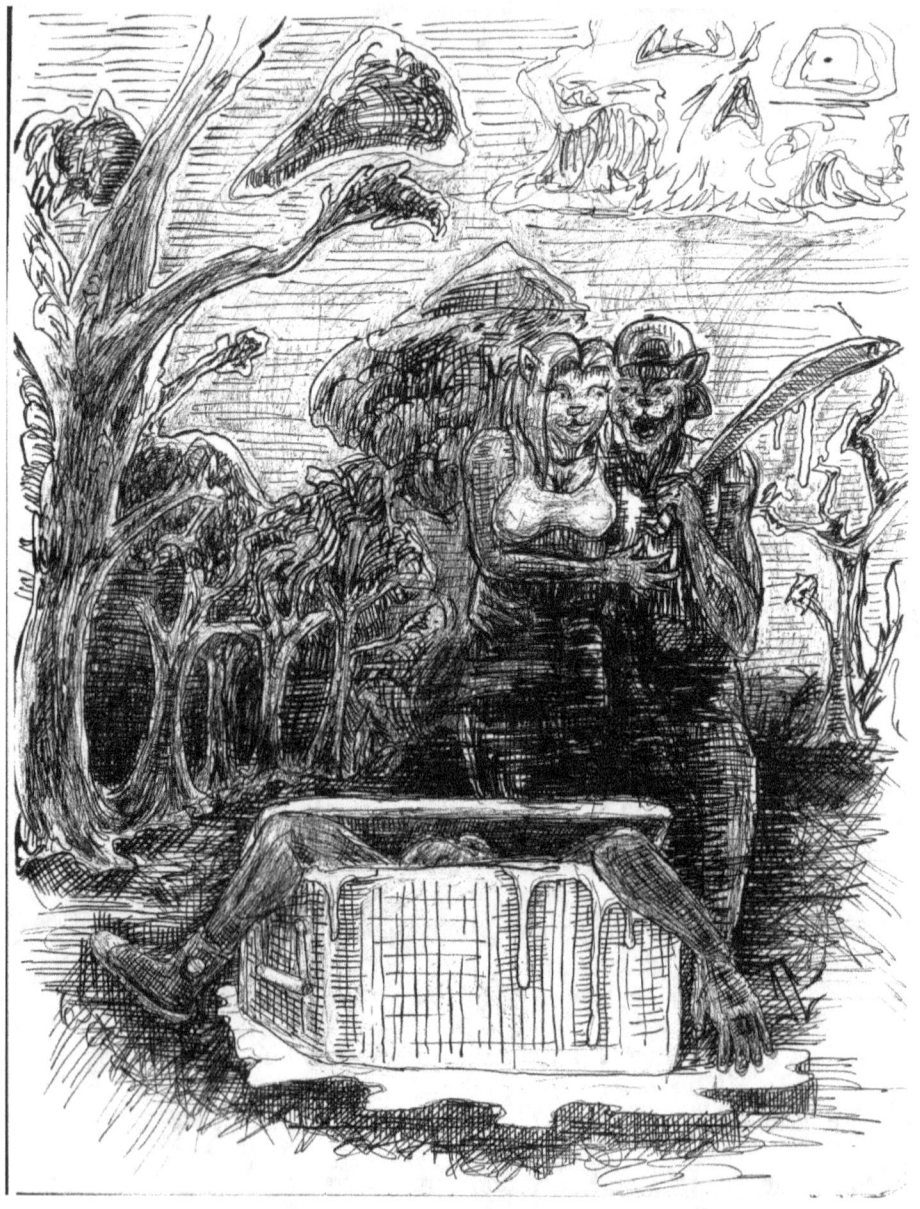

The Place I Say Goodbye

Do I hate myself? Does my self hate my eyes?

To whom do I tell all my self-loathing lies?

A pure heart is easy to trick, can be played like a fiddle,

A good soul will stay sick, a victim of this life's riddle,

A life filled with disdain, directed entirely inside,

Turns a good mind insane, where demons reside,

If I have been taught anything from what I've seen,

It's that true wrath is brought, hardest on a spirit unclean,

If I have the divine spark, then have I seen it all?

Or do I bear the beasts' mark, an angel destined to fall?

I have one last query, with perhaps no answer,

Why am I so weary, feeling like such a cancer?

Will there ever be a day, when I see myself as I see you?

Or will I always fly away, running from what is true?

I look in the mirror, and what do I see?

My own twisted reflection, glaring back at me,

I can never look for long, until I avert my gaze,

Everything I do feels wrong, wandering about a maze,

What I see in the mirror, wells up disgust in my heart,

Do I see myself clear, when I want to tear my flesh apart?

If I could have one wish granted, before I finally die,

Have a seed from a rose planted, in the place I say goodbye

Where the Creator Resides

Please conceive how dreams are haunting you,

Perceive the demons that are taunting you,

As the sun rises in the west and falls to the east,

I always do my best but end up falling to my knees,

Do I deceive? Do I lie to you?

Do as you please as the sky remains blue,

Where's the gratitude? For it wasn't always this way,

Call forth the attitude, so you can hear what I say,

I don't scare, I don't flaunt,

I become bare and ever gaunt,

The evil of the earth, roaming around,

It's the rebirth of that horrible sound,

Is it profound? What you found?

The bride wears the gown,

So the groom can tear her down,

Is it done, are you through?

Do you see that fun consumes?

Do you sense the fumes?

Or can you see refrains abuse?

If you're not ready to hear, then why are you here?

My dear, no wonder you live in constant fear,

It's near; the end which is nigh,

Bend the knee to the most high,

Will you last?

Or will you pass?

The torch of pain to the children you will gain,

Is it vain? Are you afraid of the truth that's plain?

Sane? Insane? I tell you they are one in the same,

Two sides of the same coin,

The fruits of your ignorance join,

You have decided to take the wrong side,

For you I can't help but cry,

Because the evil one does despise,

The location of where the creator resides

\

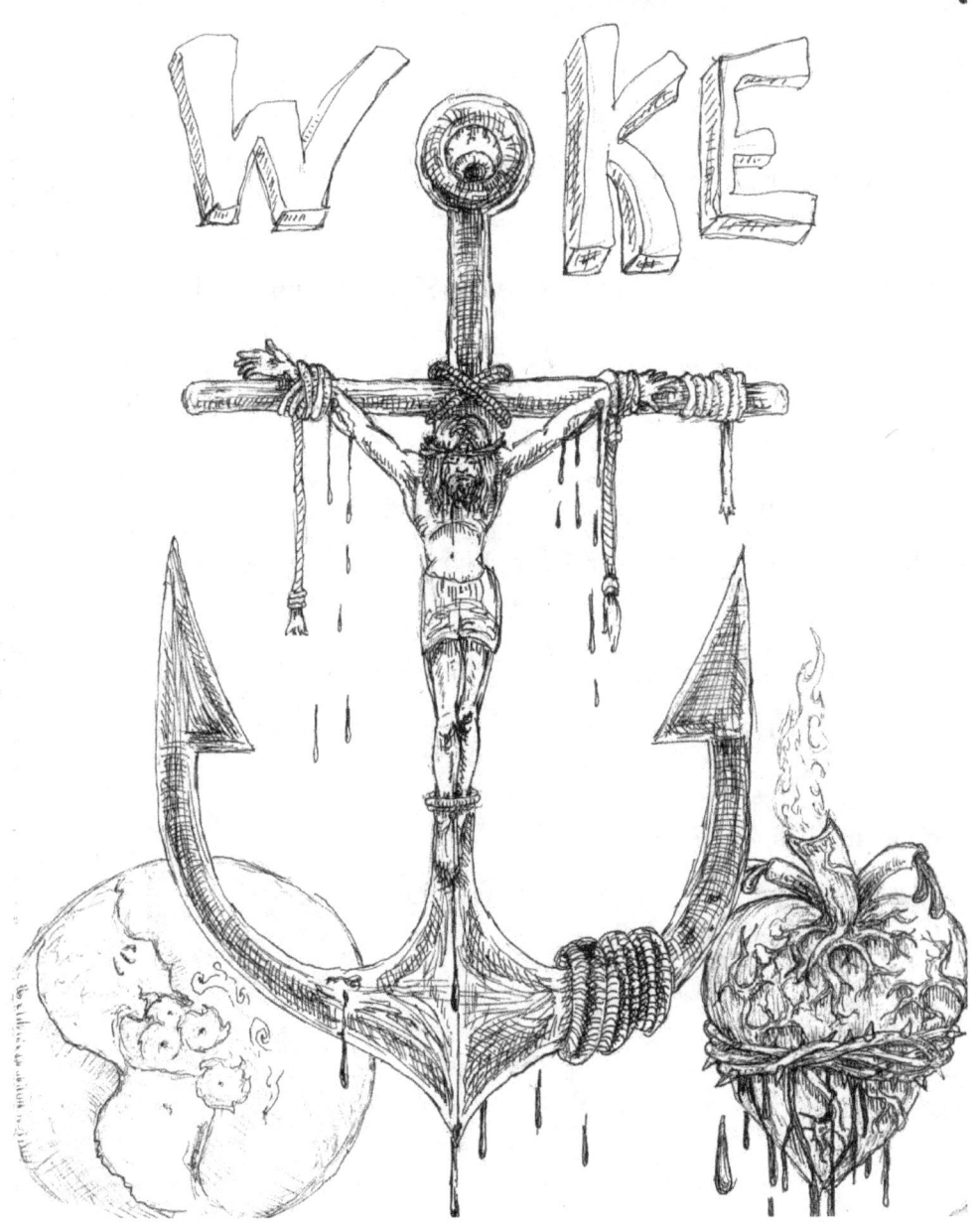

Stapled Shut

I'm grateful for this, I'm grateful for that,

My life could be much worse, and that's a fact,

Hypnotize with lies and prey on your peers,

Shared experience, trauma ties, joined fears,

Perhaps they won't be able to sense the evil lurking behind green
eyes,

Of course, this fable is about such people's upheaval and eventual
demise,

No one hears my cries, for my lips are stapled shut,

In Hells fire I'm not granted release, I have no such luck,

Tell me something I do not know, tell me something I wish to learn,

Tell me that it isn't impossible for me to find the answer for which I
yearn,

I know the difference between a truth and a lie,

That's simply a lie that I perpetuate within my mind

Suicide, what a terrible act one commits against oneself. My dear friend, the one who drew the illustrations for this book, says that suicide releases a great sorrow upon the world. I came to believe long ago that suicide does many things, but one thing it does not do is put an end to the pain that initiated it. Who knows what happens to the person who commits suicide? None of us truly do, but we all know that the pain is simply transferred to the loved ones, in this way the pain actually multiplies. Sure, the suicidal person no longer has to deal with the sorrow and suffering of the world, but their family and friends have to deal with it in addition to the gut wrenching knowledge that their loved one felt so alone and hopeless that they thought the only solution was to end their own life.

Suicide has been around as long as man himself has been. In some ancient cultures suicide was viewed as clear rebellion against the Gods, since man was property to the Gods and life and death was decided by them. In ancient Rome, suicide was viewed as a way for one to maintain honor, or had economic motives as one who is in debt can avoid the government taking their assets if they killed themselves prior to arrest thus allowing their estates to pass to their heirs. Suicide was also viewed as a way for a widow to follow his or her spouse into the afterlife. Today we view suicide as a permanent solution to a temporary problem, the act itself is condemned and the person committing the act is viewed with pity and empathy.

I have attempted suicide 3 or 4 times myself and have been sent to many psych wards for suicidal thoughts, sometimes I am sent there against my will and at times I volunteered to go. My last attempt was in 2018, I made a vow in 2019 to never try to take my own life again after the death of my father and seeing how much pain it caused those closest to him. I have had many friends take their own life, and it turns out that in my experience the illustrator of this book is indeed correct about the great sorrow suicide creates. When I ponder what my dear friends must have been going through in the days and moments leading up to their last act, I can't help but wonder what I could have done differently. I think this is a normal reaction that many of us who have known people who successfully took their own lives go through. Of course, there probably is nothing we could have done differently. At the very least we will never know, and it doesn't benefit to ponder such things, but as humans we naturally do.

To anyone out there who has suffered from suicidal ideations, talk about it because it certainly helps. The same goes to those who have lost loved ones to suicide, talk about it because you're not alone. I believe in the good Lord above, and I believe he sent his only Son to conquer this world for us. Jesus took death's power away; death has no hold over us any longer. This faith I have obtained has made it all the easier for me to stay true to my vow of not committing suicide. I don't fear death, I fear not accomplishing whatever God created me to do. We all have a purpose; we all have gifts given by our creator. Some of us were put here to teach, to heal, to be of service; but all of us were put here for a purpose. I used to be ruled by countless irrational fears, and some that make good sense (sharks); now I have one major fear that dominates my psyche: to reach the full potential that God hid within me. Who we are meant to be is inside of us all, we have the easy job: to unleash the full potential hidden within our hearts and minds.

Chaos Creep

The chaos creep within the seed,

Has the illusion of being rooted deep,

But the puss weeps and we see,

That it was always shallow as we reap,

The shallow tide could reveal the truth,

While I wallowed and cried, I was blind to you,

To my creator, and to my love,

I couldn't save her, I looked above,

Maybe she will search for you in desperation, maybe she'll try,

You saved me from trepidation, so it's to your glory I set my eyes,

God of all whom is within us all,

Each time I fall you answer the call,

Winter, summer, spring, and fall,

Wither, lumber, seethe, and stall

Judge the Sludge

Judge the sludge that slides through my veins,

Trudge through the grudge right to your grave,

A litany of sympathy,

Leads to,

The slithering epitome,

Of self-inflicted misery,

Glide through the stars,

Or get as high as mars,

You think this is how freedom tastes,

But then bow to the fiendom state,

The line in the sand was drawn before,

But in your hand the maw begs for more,

So the line is erased with the sweep of a foot and moved further along,

You quicken the pace as you weep trying to soothe your life gone wrong,

Lower and lower I sink, and I plunge,

Slower and slower, breathe in the lung,

As my soul grows closer to the devils' clutch,

The spiral seems to be viral, contagious and such,

Everyone all around me relies on a crutch,

Have I infected my peers?

Or have they enjoyed my jeers?

Or have each one of us latched onto immortalities leer?

Will I have a chance to dance?

Or be pierced by your lance?

A trance?

That sounds better to me,

Anything other than continuing to be,

To be or not to be,

That is the query.

It's this very thought of which I am weary,

It leaves my insecurities and horror glaring,

Those two monstrosities are quite the pairing,

And each of my atrocities leaves pedestrians staring,

I think that my actions look daring,

But of course they are not,

I found chaos when peace is what I sought,

Although I had no idea, not even a thought,

True Relief

I imagine that there must be a solution out of this mess,

Is this all that waits: jails, institutions, and death?

Suicide or oblivion were the two choices of all my existence,

Despite the urges for me to live with their consistent persistence,

Of what I am there is nothing, so suicide made sense,

And oblivion was appealing,

Now that I'm on the other side of the fence,

I finally see with what I'm dealing,

And I realize the monster of offense,

Reels and feeds on my feelings,

The human condition manifests in infinite ways,

We have little decision on what vice it plays,

But my malady is fatal and we suffer then die,

It is now I see it's never too late to open my eyes,

God, the universe, the essence of love,

Call it what you want but don't call it above,

I couldn't cure this disease,

That ensured my dis-ease,

But when I look for something outside of me,

I can find a daily reprieve,

And discover true relief

Sea of Gray

The dream in which we reside,

Seems to have us hypnotized,

They tell us this and they tell us that,

Ignorance is bliss, a lie they pass as fact,

I lay awake and night and sympathize,

With those who sleep through the lies,

I see their eyes when I sleep at night,

By instinct, at first I weep then I fight,

It's distinct, their faces draped in fright,

It's a symptom that they hear,

But refuse to listen to the end that's near,

Are you with them?

Do you see the blood glisten?

With its red hue,

Can you see the blue?

How about the green? Most of us live in the gray,

See what I've seen, and you'll join me in my dismay,

Welcome to the fray, you know the sort,

We should start to pray, a fitting last resort

Words I Say

The words I say crumble like wisps in the wind,

To this day I grumble at all the hearts I see worn thin,

Tell me I'm enough, and I'll choose to live as such,

But why is it someone else's love that is my crutch?

I refuse to be used, I know my worth, and it is more than that,

So why do I trudge forth as if I have forgotten that fact?

I learned my lesson and swore no person would ever hold that power,

This still doesn't lessen the gore that I accept as my soul cowers,

I don't need you, or him, or jeers,

The one that is true, is right here,

God is always around and within,

So when I frown I frown at him,

He is in me and a part of my every fiber,

Yet I still have an incessant urge to fight her,

That's done, I know me, and I really do see,

That if she wants to be won through fighting,

Then she clearly isn't the one right for me,

So this is goodbye, I thought we could fly,

I won't accept a lie, now that truth has graced my eyes

A common theme in many of my poems is that we reap what we sow. I do believe that in this life what goes around comes around, karma if you will. I don't necessarily know if karma lines up with my Christian faith, but I lean towards no. The bible, however, does mention how one reaps what he sows numerous times. In general, those who do good works will receive good rewards of the spirit and those who do evil works will in turn suffer great spiritual distress. I don't believe the term means that if we do good we'll be rich in material wealth for the riches of this world are fickle, and can be lost or even taken from us. I do believe in my own experience, however, which is that when I do good I feel good, and when I do bad I feel bad.

There's a saying in many 12 step fellowships that states that the best way to build self-esteem is by engaging in estimable acts. I mentioned before that the right way to live is etched into all of our hearts and minds, this is the conscience. Regardless of what you believe in, what faith you have, or what God you worship, most of us can agree that whatever Higher Power is out there wants us to do the right thing and does not want us to cause pain to our fellow man. Luckily for anyone reading this, you don't have to try to live a life where you lie, cheat, and steal; I have already lived that life and if you are willing to learn from my experience you can learn that it doesn't matter if you are poor or rich, popular or not, when you don't do the right thing you don't feel good about yourself and it will catch up with you.

I lied my whole life because I feared that if people knew the truth about me they wouldn't like me. Someone once told me I have the M&M syndrome: meaning I compare my outer shell to everyone else's. I see myself as the red M&M and I see all these M&M' s of different colors and compare myself to them and see them as better, but I forget that on the inside we're all the same color. Most of the things I've lied about, such as my own emotions and impulsive thoughts, are things that most people can relate to. The cheating, well that also comes from the path of deceit, for instead of being honest with myself about whether or not I'm ready for a relationship or being honest with my partner about my emotional needs I stuff it down and ignore it. When thoughts and emotions are bottled up and ignored, they will burst through and the behaviors that follow will seek to meet the needs that are ignored in any way possible. As far as stealing, well I haven't really been one to steal from people, I always stole from companies because of some narrative in my head that the companies are evil and I hurt no one by stealing a stick of deodorant. I still don't like corporate America, but I have learned that stealing is detrimental to my spirit, and it doesn't please God.

I've never tried to live my life without lying, even about my own emotions. I've lived life without cheating and without stealing, but in the end if I'm lying those two things wait at the end of the tunnel. So here's a toast to no longer answering the question 'how are you?' with an 'I'm fine', or 'good' but with an honest answer such as 'I've been having thoughts of using' or 'I'm lonely' or on a good day 'I'm content with what I have even if I am struggling at times'. Here's to supporting one another, and admitting when we are wrong. Here's to loving your family, loving your friends, and loving your enemies; even if, at times, you don't like any of them. Here's to turning over a new leaf even if it is scary. I've been living as if I'm scared there's something poisonous waiting on the other side of the leaf, but once I turned it over, I realized I've been living on the poisonous side and the side that I feared was the side that the sunlight shines upon.

Through You

Invaluable are the lessons you gave me,

Forcing me to turn to the one, who can save me,

You imparted upon me this gift,

Turning to the path allowing me to live,

The path to awareness that I am nothing,

A speck with undeserving love,

I always knew the essence out there loved me,

I couldn't deny when I looked above,

Of myself I am a sinner,

But after you arrived, I saw my heart,

So maybe I begin here,

At the point my delusion is ripped apart,

Christ you dwell inside,

All I had to do is open the door with a crooked smile,

At night, you are my light,

I welcome your love now it just took my soul a while,

The afflicted are those you call,

Not one apostle perfect,

Addicted, deserving to fall,

Now I strive for love through service,

The greatest example of the power of service was God incarnate as man,

Now I will choose to live as either a hermit or serving as much as I can,

For you, the truth, the only reprieve from this victim of self-abuse,

The one that I was, finding any excuse I could just to use,

If not through you who is the way,

I'd have to pay for my deeds,

Now I hit my knees to pray,

Fully believing you answer my pleas

Behind These Eyes

Headstrong, defiance lives in my soul,

The dead's song, a lion's den takes its toll,

Is it dreads tongs that lifts me from the liars' lull?

It's my innate refusal to budge,

That creates the sludge through which I trudge,

A grudge? No indeed,

It's revenge that allows me to continue to breathe,

A double edge for it's also the creature taking bits of me,

My spirit chiseled as if a statue is formed,

Unbeknownst to others is the monster with no limits of pockets bored,

Which keeps all of my misdeeds stored,

There's the building of a storm I am eager to release,

But I must wait for my enemies to collect for it will also destroy me,

With no promise that I will ever resurrect,

I must ensure the blast is worth the destruction that my will can direct,

Anger? Please that hardly describes,

The nature of the seas of rage that lay behind these eyes

Vessel

I have much to confess, I've never done this before,

I may struggle to not digress, I write only to write more,

The confession, of my profession, my purpose on earth,

The procession, of my deflection, developed since birth,

This may come as a surprise, likely to cause shock and awe,

A speech impediment, never understood, thoughts that clawed,

So it is natural for one to wonder, how I have come to use words,

Those shake the soul like thunder, enough to break deceits curse,

An attempt to wake children from slumber, even at their worse,

I am simply a vessel, so wonderfully made,

Formerly an imbecile, from the ashes I came,

The next riddle, many scratch their heads to solve,

How did this dismal man find such powerful resolve?

Someone deemed doomed, damaged beyond repair,

Hell on earth loomed, as I became fond of the snare,

Completely beyond reach, of any human aid,

But Jesus chose to teach, despite the serpents' escapade,

If he could endure, pain I cannot even fathom,

I have the urge, to brave the darkest cavern,

Will I face ridicule and persecution? You bet I will,

God will turn it to fuel, his execution, marvelous still,

Everything works in his plan, to my undying fascination,

And although I am only a man, I am reminded of salvation,

I'm no more special than any other child of God,

I am simply a vessel, so save your wild applause,

I've done nothing to earn this; it doesn't seem I deserve it,

As I attempt to stay earnest, I have known love, I serve it,

God is love, and God is truth, if some power claims otherwise,

Use your intuition to see through, all evils many lies

Recipe of Chaos

The masses victimized, mass reduction,

Evil truly epitomized, Satan's seduction,

Full temptation,

Of every nation,

New world order, phases began in secret,

Made up national border, the everlasting beacon,

Enemy on the rise, with constant thought,

Of humanities demise, and pain we've brought,

Is this a blessing or more of a curse?

I tend to think they're one in the same,

One being able to see the best and the worse,

To realize I'm so out of my mind makes me sane,

The recipe so full of chaos,

Is it a burden or a gift?

I see how they try to play us;

They create an illusory rift,

Maybe the words I write,

Will be the perfect potion,

To allow the oppressed to unite,

Set God's angels in motion,

The only way they can keep us down,

Is to keep us blind,

So we don't realize the true crown,

Can survive any lie,

Anything that is gained in this life, is as good as rotten fruit,

Rust has overtaken the knife, what was once pretty has no use,

We are only permitted to stay, for the blink of an eye in eternity,

For all of our souls I pray we realize we'll shrink in our uncertainty,

Only then do we finally know,

Our significance to our divine creator,

Then no matter where we go,

We fear nothing, not even the first traitor

You

I wander in wonder, as I ponder your face,

Dreading the day that we fade away,

I know I'll fail to keep the pace with your grace,

And I'll have to live through a final embrace,

Will I ever reveal these words from inside?

Maybe I'll seal it, to read after we say goodbye,

I can't predict the future but have grown use to the pain of night,

I never knew, how could I, that darkness could be so bright,

No sight, a plight of blight,

A virus that spreads,

I've always said,

Everything has an end,

Everything I touch withers and dies,

You say it's a lie but can't tell me why,

I hope it's different this time,

The seduction of destruction invades every time,

It doesn't matter on whose side,

We possess beautiful minds,

But these are the ones that so often cry,

I'm locked behind walls of steel and don't know what's real,

Each time I think I know myself a new shade of black is revealed,

All that I lack is rolled out like an onion that's been peeled,

Kneel? Yes that may help,

But then I'd have to surrender the fight with myself,

Then how would I be entertained?

The sweet isn't so without salt, the same is with pain,

I love you already, how pathetic,

I may be meddling but also prophetic,

That's how it seems when my mind,

Rips at the seams, to chaos I'm resigned,

I can't tell if you exist or are a dream from my mind,

Too good to be true?

Of course, it's you

I've been in three serious relationships; I've dated other girls here and there, but never longer than a month, and rarely with a label. At the point of each breakup it felt like my world was coming to an end, and for the next undetermined amount of time I always think that there is no one left out there for me. Each time I am surprised when I find my next love, for she seems like an even greater fit than the previous usually in ways that I never could have comprehended. It took about two years after the first ex, a year and a half after my ex-wife, and we're still in that period after my last ex and it's been over three years.

I won't say that I'm not over her, I managed to get over the hump sometime last year, but I will say that it's still difficult to imagine a better match. Getting past my mistakes with her has been the main challenge, not getting over the relationship itself. I cheated on her, lied to her, constantly chose drugs over her; these memories serve as reminders of who I was, and who I never want to be in a relationship again. Now I try to view the experience as an opportunity for learning, learning how not to treat someone you love. My heart tells me that my previous experiences will continue on and that although right now it seems impossible to imagine someone better, someone who is a better match will cross my path. My mind tells me that I may have really screwed up this time, and that I'll be alone forever. My mind, however, is sick. My heart is not sick, so I have to trust my gut and what God tells me. God tells me to be patient, and to pray for all the right things and to pray for guidance towards the path of kindness. I truly believe that if I am patient and continue to do the next right thing, someone will organically cross my path, and I will be able to enjoy my next relationship the right way. Right now, I think it's God's will that I stay single and continue to work on myself; I'm grateful for the opportunity, truly.

Alive to Serve

In it creeps, the subtle freeze,

Capable of bringing the strong to their knees,

Not even the strongest of us all,

Can withstand the predestined fall,

Who was I to think our love was eternal,

We were on the brink, our love was inferno,

Were we both the fool? Or did you know all along?

I'm simply a tool, a vessel to sing a sad song,

The sadness rings, throughout my lonely halls,

My heart sings, bouncing off all the walls,

Where did you go, I thought we were bound to last,

How could I know? That the sound was a man aghast,

My fatal flaw, was that I believed what you said,

I sit in awe, shocked that you actually fled,

Frozen stone cold in my tracks, unable to move past this mistake,

I now see all that I lack; I was ignorant to what was at stake,

How did this come to be? Why was I caught off guard?

As I writhe and bleed, I look ahead to the bright star,

All I can do now, is pray you get what you deserve,

So as I take a bow, I must trudge on, alive to serve

Travis Johnston

The Abyss of our Sinful Whims

The pit, the bottomless abyss of each of our sinful whims,

That's it, the seamless stitch that teach each of us of the cyst,

That blight which seems to always persist to exist,

All consuming, the progression,

Much assuming of the obsession,

The righteous fuming, causing depression,

With all its rambling digression,

Always ending in repression,

Spoken in a deadly precession,

Everything I touch will wither and die,

Call it the touch of Mitus,

I look to the sky and scream why,

Why must our mind fight us?

My heart and mind are never on the same page,

Resisting the guarantee of change,

It's quite deranged,

Teetering on the edge of the sane and insane,

Was I like this at birth? Is this what they call fate?

Anywhere I go on earth, I can't escape my own face,

It's this bitter taste that I have learned to hate,

We try to outrun our shadows, but instead there we are,

Ending in death or in the gallows, either way we don't get far,

In the end, my soul will break or bend,

To whom will I send the lie that pretends?

Pretends to know the pretense,

Of the mind,

Me? I say I'm fine,

But I'm not,

My stomachs in a knot,

With blood clots,

Is this real? Or simply a projection of my conscience?

I can't feel, as for my humanity, I've seemed to have lost this

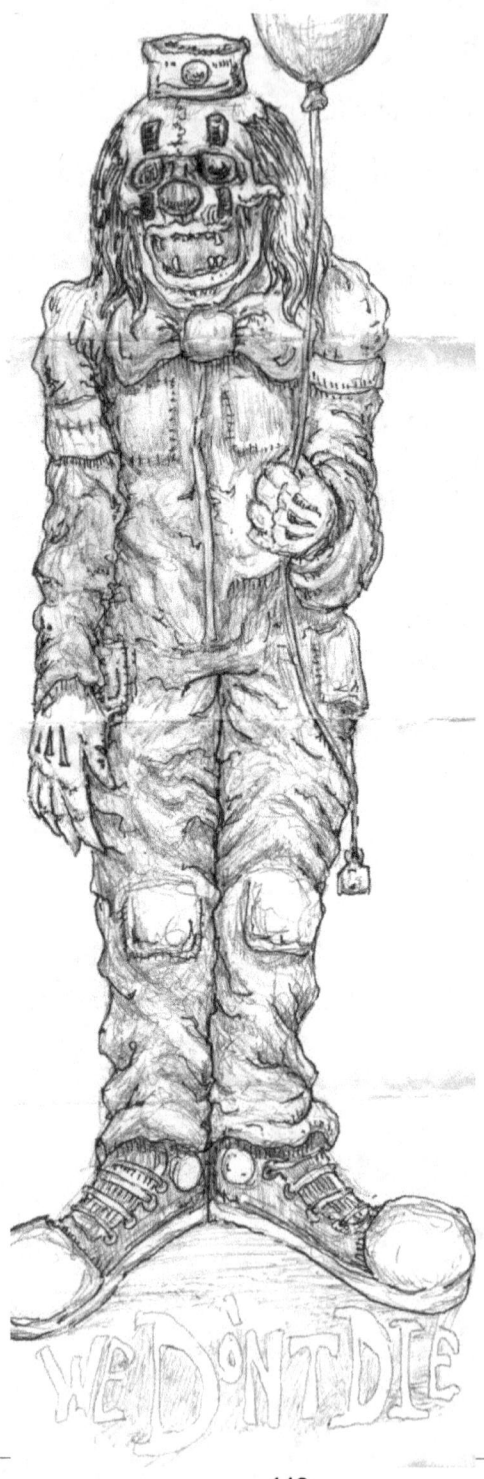

The Worm

I wiggle and squirm, like the lowest of all creatures on earth,

Lower than dirt, the worm, not what my mother foresaw at birth,

I never meant to be a burden, a constant source of worry,

My own filth, I lurch in, lower than the critters that scurry,

At least they are fulfilling their purpose,

The reason they were put here,

I spend my life the recipient of curses,

From enemies and those I hold dear,

If you would ask what I think,

I would tell you I earned this pain,

As I inch onward to the brink,

I see I'm the weak link of the chain,

I seem to always bring others down,

They say misery hates to be alone,

Wishing that I could be home bound,

This lie I have made my own,

If I choose to cast out the lies,

I would be forced to speak the truth,

My internal anguish always supplies,

The little voice that causes self-abuse,

Must I speak my agony aloud?

For everyone to be enticed to hear?

Is my heavenly father proud?

Or does condemnation draw ever near?

Anguish, chaos, deception, my worst enemy my reflection,

Squeamish, slay us, inception, a downward spiral my direction,

Do I yearn for well wishes, to be handed any charity?

No, I will reject any kisses, and avoid any gifted clarity

The Most High

All these talks of empty glasses, broken dreams, abstract thoughts,

Hypnosis subjugating the masses, broken seams, horror wrought,

The stitches of reality withering like a candle, lit the entire night,

The onset of max calamity, a snake to handle, true deceits might,

I am not the one to decipher the code burned into the bloody knife,

We all face the piper, our insides churned, by deaths coming scythe,

Eternal life in this flesh suit, here in this mortal coil,

Which does not really exist,

I feel I'd be better off mute, my insides destined to boil,

Leading to pain that persists,

My eyes are meant to fall victim to my brain that is ill,

Sickened with thoughts contrarily true,

God takes people and picks them, to be used in his will,

Disown my thinking, self-reliance is through,

Today it's far too easy to fall victim to self-hate,

Self-seeking doesn't please me, I realized too late,

I know there's only one way, for the damage to be relieved,

I must admit each day; the most high is my only reprieve

I've met many people whose primary drug of abuse is meth, as is mine. Most of the people I meet that have abused meth in their past claim that one of the most enticing effects is a spike in creativity. They claim that the energy and focus methamphetamine use provides allows them to write more and better songs, to paint or draw better, or perform any other creative feat with greater ease and precision. This has never been my experience.

My father died in a motorcycle accident in late August 2019; I had never written a poem prior to his death. I ended up relapsing for a couple of weeks after his death, and in September of that same year I went to rehab for the second time. While in rehab I wrote my first poem, and realized it was quite good. I wrote several more while there and have continued to write since then. Usually when I'm using drugs I don't even try to write poetry, because I have always had this innate idea that what I write comes from my Higher Power. You could take any of the poems in this book and I promise you none of them took over ten minutes, most of them took under five. When I write, it just flows out of my mind, there is hardly ever a time where I have to pause to figure out how to rhyme or what word should come next.

During one relapse an Uncle of mine was trying to encourage me to find myself again which he hoped would get me to try to get sober once more. My uncle recommended that I try writing a poem even though I was under the influence. I remember writing the poem, and I remember noticing that it was just requiring too much thought. I finished it, and it was ok but really not that good. The reason is clear to me now, and at the time of writing it I already had an idea of the reason it wouldn't be great; the reason is that (and I truly believe this) this is a gift given to me by my creator and when I am under the influence of the artificial Higher Power known as meth I am shut off from the sunlight of my Creator. My mind doesn't allow God to enter in with inspiration. Perhaps it is because of shame, or perhaps it's simply that I really am a different person when I am using. I highly doubt that it's because God *can't* get through, for I believe that anything is possible for God, and God has granted me moments of clarity while using so I could see a way out and get back to recovery.

To be honest, I'm glad I can't enjoy one of my favorite pastimes and write while I'm high because that in itself is one of my greatest motivations for staying sober. When I feel like using meth or drinking I simply start writing, in fact that's why I wrote this excerpt. When faced with a craving or an urge and I begin to write, I am reminded that this is not something I can enjoy doing while under the influence. If that isn't a gift from God, I don't know what is!

Terrible Dimensions

On this voyage he will embark, braving tremendous seas,

Always surrounded by the dark, where courage is conceived,

They say the best of each seafarer, is not made in calm waters,

After all the greatest cross bearer, faced countless plotters,

They say what doesn't kill you,

Serves to add inner strength,

So turn from what will thrill you,

For honor go any length,

This is the only thing,

The sailor can never lose to the sea,

Relying on God will bring,

Strength nobody can relieve,

Perhaps it is this lack of perception,

The one making us effectively blind,

That is the cause of black deception,

The land bounds an endless bind,

When there is but a boat of wood,

And an endless void at every turn,

If I could show you I would,

But from experience most must learn,

I suppose this is truly meant to be,

That we cannot learn from another's mistake,

I cannot give what wasn't leant to me,

I cannot convince you of what's at stake,

All I can do is meditate on each word,

And do my best to plant a seed,

Because even in this hateful evil world,

I hope that you'll someday see,

This is something, for which I pray,

For we all deserve what the seafarer has,

Perhaps on each of our final days,

We can see salvation runs a different path,

One last line must be written,

To speak of the gnawing teeth, the terrible dimensions,

If this world has you smitten,

Remember the road to hell is paved with good intentions

What God Says

Temptation for me,

Is the sensation of glee,

But this is a mirage,

Surely a façade,

For in my bones, I already know this path,

I am tempted by it and where it goes in fact,

I may be under attack, by the paralysis of my body at night,

I see the devil's tact; it's this analysis, which is the light,

How else shall I fight?

This world and the evil that it breeds,

Shows me that through God I can believe,

I can handle this existence with ease,

Only with persistence and the Lords' reprieve,

It is through work, and prayer,

For at times I lurk in despair,

After all this is Lucifer's world,

So I mustn't forget God's word,

When I feel condemned, I know I am victim,

To none other than Beelzebub's deceit,

For in the end when I choose to listen,

I know what God says about me

Well, you made it to the end! Whoever you are, I hope that the poetry moved you, and I hope the entries in between didn't bore you too much. My dream is that someday I can devote all of my time to writing, although it is hard for me to believe that this dream will ever be realized. I pray that someone out there, even if it is only one person, has been helped in some way. Perhaps this person found someone or some words that they can relate to, perhaps this person feels less alone now. I don't know if anyone will be helped, but I pray that someone is because that is the purpose of me publishing this book. I have no delusions that I'll become rich or famous. To me it doesn't matter whether I do or not because, as previously stated, that is not why I took on this project.

If I was given the option to pick one point I want people to take away from all of this it would be this: no pain or sorrow, no difficulty or shortcoming, no mistake or failure cannot be turned into something beautiful. I only really write good poetry when I am in pain, for pain makes me passionate. I am only motivated to attempt new projects when I have just overcome some suffering, or when I am in the middle of said suffering. Turn to God, be of service, do everything out of love.

To quote my favorite verse in the bible, 1 Corinthians 13:4-8 "Love is patient and kind; love does not envy or boast; it is not arrogant or rude. It does not insist on its own way; it is not irritable or resentful; it does not rejoice with wrongdoing but rejoices with the truth." Most of my problems come from me living with a spirit of fear; countless fears have plagued me and led me to seek relief from this fear at any cost. Love drives out all forms of fear; so love yourselves, love your neighbors, and love your enemy. We all need love desperately, and in my experience, only through love can we conquer the demons that plague our thoughts and minds!

www.ingramcontent.com/pod-product-compliance
Lightning Source LLC
Chambersburg PA
CBHW062322290526
45794CB00005B/1861